1 MONTH OF
FREE
READING

at
www.ForgottenBooks.com

By purchasing this book you are
eligible for one month membership to
ForgottenBooks.com, giving you
unlimited access to our entire
collection of over 1,000,000 titles via
our web site and mobile apps.

To claim your free month visit:

www.forgottenbooks.com/free921694

ISBN 978-0-260-00613-4
PIBN 10921694

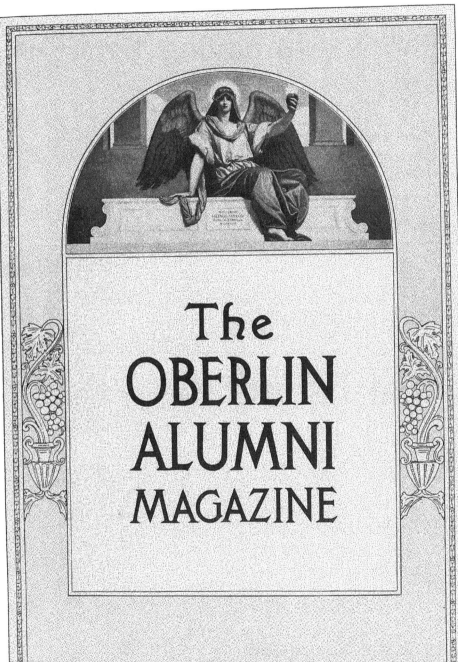

The OBERLIN ALUMNI MAGAZINE

VOL. XIX   JULY, 1923   No. 10

The Oberlin Alumni Magazine

Member of Alumni Magazines, Associated

Published monthly, except in August and September, by
THE ALUMNI ASSOCIATION OF OBERLIN COLLEGE
WILLIAM S. AMENT, '10, Editor and Manager

Subscriptions—Per year for United States and Canada and including Membership in the Alumni Association, $3.50; elsewhere, $3.75; Subscription alone, $2.50 and $2.75 as above; Single copies, 25 cents.

Communications intended for publication should be sent to W. S. Ament, Alumni Office, Oberlin, Ohio. They should be in hand before the 15th to insure attention for the issue of the succeeding month.

Remittances and advertising copy should be sent to the same address. Checks should be made payable to "The Alumni Association of Oberlin College." National Advertising Representative, Roy Barnhill, Inc., 23 E. 26th St., New York City.

Entered as second class matter at the post office, Oberlin, Ohio, under Act of Congress of March 3, 1879.

The Alumni Association

OF OBERLIN COLLEGE

The Last Chance

This is the last issue of the Alumni Magazine on the Class Subscription Plan. All non-subscribers in the classes listed below who wish to take advantage of the $2 rate should send in their subscriptions immediately.

The offer closes September 1.

AS A MEMBER OF

THE ALUMNI ASSOCIATION OF OBERLIN COLLEGE

AGREE TO PAY THE ASSOCIATION DUES AS MARKED

			Mark Here
I	Founders' Membership	$500.00 or more	$------
II	Sustaining Membership	$100.00 or more	------
III	Life Membership, one payment . .	$50.00	------
IV	Life Membership, six annual payments of 10.00		------
	The above do not include Magazine subscription		
V	Contributing Membership and Alumni Magazine one year . . .	$5.00	$------
VI	Membership and Alumni Magazine one year	$3.50	$------
VII	Membership alone . . .	$2.50	$------
VIII	Alumni Magazine alone	$2.50	$------
IX	Alumni Magazine alone on Class Subscription Plan . . .	$2.00	$------
	Total . . .		$------

Name   Class

Address

Date

Subscription price

$2.50

or on the Class Plan at

$2.00

which applies to new subscribers in the following classes: 1875, 1876, 1885, 1898, 1901, 1904.

The Oberlin Alumni Magazine

Volume XIX, Number 10   Oberlin, Ohio, July, 1923

The Oberlin Building and Endowment Campaign

THE GREAT OPPORTUNITY FOR OBERLIN ALUMNI

The announcement of the Oberlin Building and Endowment Campaign for $4,500,000 marks the 90th Commencement as an epoch in the life of Oberlin College.

Launched by the trustees to meet vital and pressing needs, unanimously approved by the Executive Committee of the Alumni Association, by the Alumni Council on February 22nd, and by the Alumni at their 84th annual meeting June 19th, and enrolling more than 1,000 former students of Oberlin College as regional and class campaign chairmen, the Campaign commands the vital interest and unflinching loyalty of every former student of Oberlin College.

To each alumnus and former student the Campaign gives a chance to repay in some degree his debt of honor and love. Oberlin College, aided by its endowment and contributions, gave to each of us education costing at least twice what we paid in tuitions. By returning some of this free gift we can preserve undiminished opportunities for the student generations to follow. But the investment of Oberlin in us is more than a financial one. Through this Campaign we can in some degree compensate the college for the gifts of knowledge, appreciation, inspiration, and friendship which we have received.

To the Alumni Association the Campaign offers the one great opportunity to create among the alumni a sense of power and solidarity which will give us a high standing among the alumni groups of the United States, and which will make an effective permanent organization possible.

To Oberlin College the failure of this campaign means mediocrity; success means leadership in the college world.

With Oberlin's emphasis on individualism the question stands: Have we the sense of team work, the fraternal spirit, the ability to support by our efforts some great cause, which will carry through this epochal undertaking?

If we are made of the right stuff, be the financial result what it may, when this Campaign is over we shall be a unified, active, competent and loyal body of more than fifteen thousand alumni and former students. This is the Alumni Association which we are attempting to create.

With such a body pledged to "carry on," the Campaign can not fail, and supported by such a group of earnest and loyal people the college faces an assured future.

TO WHOM IT MAY CONCERN

A Continuing City

"The individual must be made by education, a citizen of a city not made with hands." I found that sentence in the London Times about a year ago. and I quote it now because it happens to express what is perhaps the chief article in my educational creed. At any rate, as I ask myself what we are aiming at in places like Oberlin, I answer that it is not primarily mental discipline, essential as that is; still less is it preparation for the business of life. Indeed, as to the second of these aims, I should like to add a new inscription to the Memorial Arch—if it were not already so admirably inscribed—that all who pass under it on their way to lecture or laboratory might read and mark and learn. It is the words of Aeneas to his son on the eve of the last battle with Turnus: "Learn from me, boy, what valour and true effort are; you may learn success from others." *Fortunam ex aliis*—not a bad motto for a college of the liberal arts, and certainly not out of place on a martyr's memorial.

For the goddess *Fortuna*, or Success, is the least stable, the lease calculable of divinities. Her wheel, that lifts and lowers at her whim those who are bound to it, has been for a thousand years the emblem of instability. But we ask another sort of symbol for our efforts; we seek a continuing city.

That is why, as I see it, we study history and literature, philosophy and science—for the relish of eternity in them. We are all at some moment of our lives, like John Stuart Mill at the crisis of his, liable to be harrowed by the Mephistophelian question: If you were now to obtain what you are so eagerly striving for, would your life be more interesting and satisfying? And most of us, I fancy, would have to say no. The truth is that satisfaction is not to be predicated of most of the occupations by which we earn our bread, and that is why it is so important that we should have other interests and other satisfactions which are not dependent upon the vicissitudes of the human lot—to which, indeed, the words success and failure do not apply. That is why it is so important that we should receive naturalization —for we are none of us born there—in the city that human hands do not fashion and can not

destroy. That is why the permanent elements in education are the only ones that ultimately matter.

Meanwhile, the superintendent of schools in Flat River, Mo., writes to the New York Eve. ning Post: "In spite of the certainty that eight-tenths of all the reading that will be done by eight-tenths of our young people in their future lives will be done in the news. papers, we continue to stress the technical points of Shakespearian drama and to discuss Burke's 'Conciliation' in our high; schools." Well, I'm not very keen about dramatic tech. nicalities myself, at least in high schools, nor do I admire dissection anywhere, being wholly of Wordsworth's mind on that subject; but I can not help wondering whether supervised newspaper reading is much more valuable. No one regrets more than I do that high school students go their way with so slight a deposit of Burke and Shakespeare in their minds. But supposing that Macbeth and the Conciliation speech were adequately presented to them, is it so certain that in the long run, even for the eight-tenths, a course in newspaper reading would render life more interesting and satisfying? Of course your answer to such a question wholly depends upon whether you really respect literature. If you don't, why, then, no doubt, a profound analysis of moral weakness, like Macbeth, shot through with stormy beauty, and a piece of final wisdom on many problems of government, like the Conciliation, will seem to you less valuable than the hasty record of the day's happenings commented upon, often, as hastily.

Ah, well, the battle of the books will never end, the irrepressible conflict between the ancients and the moderns. Somewhere in the no-man's land between the warring hosts, I dare say, lies the truth. Burke and the newspapers, Shakespeare and the cinema—put in that way, I suppose that no man who has "discourse of reason" could possibly pronounce the second alternative. But I grant that to put it in that way is hardly fair.

Charles H. A. Wager

The Campaign

The great event of the Alumni Meeting, which is for the most part reported elsewhere, was the announcement of the Campaign for $4,500,000 which is planned for the month of November.

Speaking on the topic "Why Oberlin needs $4,500,000" President King summarized the conditions at Oberlin which make this great united effort imperative. His points were essentially as follows:

INCOME IS DIMINISHED

In 1917-18 Oberlin College received its first income from the bequest of the late Charles M. Hall. The amount of the income for that year was $184,000, most of which was used for the first increase in the excessively low faculty salary scale of that period, and the remainder for the excess expenditure over other income. In 1919-20, when the income from the bequest reached its high point, $196,500, a second, larger increase in the salary scale was made, bringing it up almost to the level of that of other first-class colleges.

The annual cost of the second increase, however, was approximately $162,000, an amount that the advance of $12,500 in the income of that year obviously did little to meet. The extra cost was temporarily met from other sources, but the College relied chiefly, in making the increase, upon confident assurances that there would soon be a great advance in the income from the Hall bequest. That expectation has not been realized. Instead, the income has fallen off, dropping from $196,-500 in 1919-20 to $137,500 in 1920-21, and then to $84,000 in 1921-22. This reduction of more than $100,000 in the income of the College has had the effect of a temporary shrinkage of a clear $2,000,000 in its capital. It has been the more serious in its results, because it came at a time when the College expected, and greatly needed, a large increase in its resources.

DRASTIC ECONOMIES PRACTICED

To meet the very difficult situation resulting from this loss, the College has taken four steps, of which some at least are very undesirable: It has cut from the annual budget, already closely restricted to actual needs, the sum of $65,000, thereby bringing to the verge of disaster certain vital needs of the College; it has doubled the charges for tuition; it has increased the number of students in the College of Arts and Sciences from 1,000 to 1,200; and it has sought five-year pledges from guarautors. With all these efforts it has not been able to avoid incurring a deficit in every year but one since 1917, and it is never free from the danger of exceeding its income, even on the present limited scale of operation. *Only a permanent increase in its resources can give final relief. Two million dollars is the irreducible minimum needed at this time.*

CAPITAL HAS SHRUNK

It is of course the hope of the College that the income from the Hall bequest will some day regain or exceed its former proportions. If it does so, the increase will all be needed to wipe out the accumulated deficit of the past few years, amounting now to about $200,000, and to restore to the working capital of the College the large sum that has in recent years become unproductive.

For a number of years it has been necessary from time to time to take income-yielding properties as sites for College buildings, and to use income-producing funds for the purchase of properties indispensable to the future development of the College plant, but incapable of yielding income at present. The funds used for these purchases, amounting to about a half-million dollars, were not restricted by their donors to any particular use, but income was greatly lessened through their transfer to non-productive but necessary uses. Although this was entirely proper, and their integrity as assets of the College is wholly unimpaired, it is still certainly desirable that the gap left in the productive capital by their transfer should be filled as soon as possible.

If the Hall bequest should again produce its former income, it would take the entire increase for a period of from five to ten years to fill this gap and wipe out the accumulated deficit.

NEW ENDOWMENT NEEDED

It is imperative, therefore, that new money for endowment be raised *at this time*, simply to restore the College to its normal level of operation and relieve it from the present necessity of depending upon annual subscriptions to meet its current expenses. For these two purposes alone the income of the $2,000,000 endowment now sought will all be needed.

Moreover, on account of the steadily advancing cost of education, there must be a corresponding enlargement of the scholarship funds, if Oberlin's opportunities are to be kept open to self-supporting students. At least $100,000 should be raised now for this purpose. And for the Conservatory of Music there is needed for general purposes an endowment of $400,000.

COLLEGE IS CRAMPED FOR ROOM

In addition to new endowment, the College urgently needs funds for new buildings. Its building program has been held up since before the war. For its most urgent, immediate needs at least $2,000,000 is imperatively required. This sum must be made to go as far as possible toward providing a modern recitation building; a college hospital; a woman's gymnasium; the theological group; laboratories for the scientific departments; dormitories, especially for men; and an addition to the library. And with every building, to prevent its becoming a drain upon the resources of the College, there should be an endowment for its upkeep.

The list of imperative needs, therefore, stands as follows·

For endowment of salary increases already made $2,000,000
For scholarship aid for self-supporting students 100,000
For the Conservatory of Music...... 400,000
For the most urgent building requirements 2,000,000

Total $4,500,000

THE NEED OF EQUIPMENT

The needs of Oberlin College from the point of view of the student were presented by Miss Ruth Savage, '23· who described the need for a women's gymnasium and swimming pool, for additional women's dormitories, and for a woman's building and recreation hall. The need for the gymnasium is especially urgent since only 624 of the 1,100 girls on the campus can secure locker space, and since all the equipment is inadequate for this large number of girls.

Mr. Malcolm Jameson, '23· stressed the need of dormitories for men, especially since the College does not encourage groups of men to provide their own fraternity houses. He also made a plea for building and equipment for the department of physics.

ALUMNI COÖPERATION

The needs of Oberlin College from the point of view of the alumni were presented by Mrs. A. F. Millikan, '93· and Grove H. Patterson, '05·

Mrs. Millikan opened her talk with a story illustrating the necessity of getting and keeping a vision in the midst of our daily work, and applied the principle to the new undertaking of Oberlin College. She spoke of the great privilege of being able to repay to Oberlin some part of the blessings that students for 90 years have received as a matter of course. She then took up four points as being essential to the carrying out of the great project: contact, conference, confidence, and coöperation. We must re-establish, through the Alumni Magazine and other means, the close contact with the college that so many of us have lost. We are already feeling and

seeing the results of conference in the splendid organization of the campaign. We must give our full confidence in return for the confidence that President King and his associates have rested in us. And finally we must all come together in a new spirit of coöperation.

Mr. Patterson restated the subject assigned to him to read "The Need of Oberlin College by the Alumni." After speaking of the wisdom of the college in putting the conduct of the campaign into the hands of a firm so efficient and capable as Tamblyn and Brown, he brought out the point that the campaign is an opportunity not only to make our united alumni body stand for something more than it has ever stood for before, but to make it stand for more than any other alumni body in the country. Lastly Mr. Patterson emphasized the "spiritual quality" as the only hope of civilization, and the fact that we must consider most of all the sources of this hope. The world is to be saved by "the translation of ideals planted in youth into action in the adult," and it is our great privilege "to support and maintain an organization which puts into the world the kind of men and women who are going to save it."

IT CAN BE DONE

In a few last words Mr. W. F. Bohn, assistant to the President, sketched the great work of organization which has already been accomplished, and recorded his belief that Oberlin College can and will raise four and a half million dollars.

IT WILL BE DONE

Immediately following this program Mr. Frank C. Van Cleef moved that the alumni pledge support to the campaign. The motion was unanimously carried.

FIVE HUNDRED THOUSAND DOLLAR CONDITIONAL GIFT

To aid Oberlin in supplying adequate funds, the General Board of Education of the Rockefeller Foundation has promised Oberlin College $500,000 on condition that an additional million and a half be raised to complete the two million dollars designated for endowment. As this is one of the largest conditional gifts ever made by the General Education Board, no effort will be spared by friends of Oberlin College to meet the conditions.

The Campaign Organization

Some conception of the magnitude of the organization which Oberlin College is forming to handle the great campaign can be obtained from the roster of chairmen, published by the National Headquarters, 537 Bulkley Building, Cleveland. Starting with Theodore E. Burton, '72, honorary national chairman, the roster lists about a thousand chairmen, representing every section of the United States and the world, and in addition a "campaign director" for each class. The most hasty survey of this roster shows such a tremendous number of fine and capable leaders that confidence in the work of the organization is inevitable.

ALUMNI CAMPAIGN MEETINGS

This formidable list of chairmen was appointed at a series of conferences, covering the entire United States and numbering sixty, at each of which President King or some other representative of Oberlin College presented the financial situation, while some member of the organization explained how the $4,500,000 is to be raised. After national and divisional conferences, the following state and district meetings were held.

STATE AND DISTRICT CONFERENCES

April 2—Connecticut—New Haven
April 3—E. Mass., Me., N. H.—Boston
April 4—W. Mass., Vt.—Springfield
April 5—Eastern New York—Albany
April 6—Central New York—Syracuse
April 12—Kansas—Topeka
April 13—Missouri—Kansas City
April 14—Minnesota, N. Dak.—Minneapolis. Wis.—Milwaukee
April 17—Illinois—Chicago
April 18—Indiana—Indianapolis
April 19—Kentucky—Louisville
April 20—Tennessee—Nashville
April 23—District 9, Ohio—Dayton
April 24—District 12, Ohio, Cincinnati
April 25—Western Pennsylvania—Pittsburgh
April 26—Eastern Pennsylvania—Philadelphia
April 27—Metropolitan N. Y.—New York City
April 28—Michigan—Detroit. Western N. Y.—Buffalo. Neb., S. Dakota—Omaha
April 30—N. and S. Carolina—Salisbury, N. C. Colorado—Denver
May 1—Ala., Ga., Miss., La.—Atlanta, Ga.
May 2—Florida—Jacksonville
May 5—So. California—Los Angeles
May 7—Virginia—Norfolk
May 8—West Virginia—Charleston
May 9—District 6, Ohio—Lima
May 11—District 10, Ohio—Columbus
May 12—Indiana—Indianapolis
May 14—Texas—Dallas. Oregon—Portland
May 16—Oklahoma. Arkansas—Tulsa, Okla. W. Washington—Seattle
May 19—Iowa—Des Moines
May 21—E. Washington—Spokane. Idaho—Boise
May 22—District 5, Ohio—Warren
May 23—District 2, Ohio—Sandusky. Montana—Billings
May 24—District 1, Ohio—Toledo
May 26—District 8, Ohio—Akron
May 29—District 7, Ohio—Mansfield
June 4—District 4, Ohio—Cleveland
June 5—District 3, Ohio—Elyria

President King's Western Trip

President King and Mr. Bohn, the Assistant to the President, returned Saturday, June 9, from an extended absence in the west, visiting alumni associations and attending conferences of alumni in preparation for the financial campaign next fall. Meetings were held at Omaha, Denver, Salt Lake City, Los' Angeles, Long Beach, Claremont, Oakland, Portland, Seattle, Spokane, and Billings.

The first meeting was at Omaha, following a thoroughly satisfactory conference in the afternoon. Oberlin men and women from Nebraska, and near by states were present. The meeting was enthusiastic and furnished a good introduction to the successful series of meetings which followed.

Large numbers of Alumni and former students attended these series of meetings and some of the occasions were made noteworthy by the presence of distinguished guests.

At Denver the newly elected Governor of Colorado, Hon. William E. Sweet, gave the official address of welcome. Chief Justice J. H. Teller, '74, gave an address

At Salt Lake City a new chapter was organized,—Oberlin men and women gathering from considerable distance in Utah and Idaho for this meeting.

There were 217 at the banquet in Los Angeles. This meeting was presided over by John F. Peck, the Associate National Chairman, for the Pacific Coast. Professor R. A. Millikan, '91, trustee of the college and President of the California Institute of Technology, introduced President King and Mr. Bohn. Among those present were Dr. Charles E. St. John, formerly Dean of the College of Arts and Sciences, now of Mt. Wilson Solar Observatory.

Smaller but very enthusiastic meetings were held at Long Beach and Claremont.

Arrangements at Oakland were in charge of Jay B. Nash of 1911. Mr. Nash is one of the outstanding influential citizens of Oakland, in charge of physical education in the public schools, playgrounds, and recreation. Mrs. John Henry Barrows was a guest of honor at this meeting.

At Portland, Seattle and Spokane there were similar meetings, attended by from 75 to 125 Oberlin men and women.

The last meeting of the series was at Bill.

Some of the 258 Seniors in the Academic Procession on the way to the
Baccalaureate Service

ings, Mont., attended by representative Oberlin men and women from Montana and Wyoming.

In addition to the alumni meetings and committee conferences which were held in these various cities, numerous addresses were given in colleges, high schools, before civic clubs, and in churches.

Since the first of March President King and Mr. Bohn have visited twenty-six states from New England to the Pacific Coast in the interests of the alumni, and in addition, Mr. Ament, Alumni Secretary, Secretary George Jones, and Professor Root have visited other alumni organizations in the east, south and middle west. Up to the present time sixty alumni conferences have been held in addition to the general alumni meetings.

COMMENCEMENT IN SHANSI

The 1923 Commencement of the Oberlin Shansi Memorial Schools falls on June 27. The speaker is to be Dr. Jacob Gould Schurman, United States Minister to China, who is even better known as the former president of Cornell University. He is making a special trip into Shansi for this purpose, and Governor Yen, widely known as the one governor in China who is strictly devoting himself to the development of his province in peace and quiet, has extended him an invitation to be his guest

during his visit in Taiyuanfu, the capital city of Shansi Province. Taiyuanfu is forty miles from Taiku, the location of the Oberlin schools, along the government road which is being kept in condition by constant supervision.

The largest classes on record will graduate from the college and the primary school, and the high school class is one of the largest to leave the institution. This high school class will be the last one to graduate from the four year high school course. The next class will have to study for two more years instead of one, and graduate from the new six-year high school.

THE REUNION GLEE CLUB CONCERT

The most enjoyable of the whole series of Reunion Glee Club concerts was directed by Jack Wirkler on Wednesday night, June 20. By omitting the usual operetta the program was brought down to a length permitting of maximum enjoyment without fatigue. The program was well-balanced between serious and humorous numbers and had the variety made possible by a combination of men's and women's voices. The fact that at the end of a long and hot Commencement season the Chapel was full for this concert proves the continuous attraction of fine choral singing, especially under the experienced direction of Jack Wirkler.

The Commencement Address

Doctor Paul Elmer More of Princeton, author of the scholarly Shelbourne Essays, delivered the commencement address on "The Demon of the Absolute." Defining the Demon of the Absolute as the reason run wild, Dr. More advanced the thesis that "Reason, which we all agree is our guide of life, must be controlled and curbed as much as our desires or our passions."

To illustrate the tendency of rationalism to swing from one extreme to the other, Dr. More first cited the history of the church. The impact of the logical abolutism of Greek philosophy upon the simple Christianity of the early centuries generated a series of heresies and forced the church at its great councils to formulate its fundamental beliefs. The essence of the Nicean creed and of the pronouncements following it, was the statement that Christ was at once human and more than human. But this statement did not satisfy the rationalists, trained as they were in the Greek dialectic. To the question, can one person have two natures, one human and one divine, they answered in the negative and created instead an absolute God of pure abstractions, entirely removed from human life and having no connection with reality.

In our own day, however, rationalism has swung to the opposite extreme, denying or ignoring the divinity in Christ and satisfying itself with naturalism gilded over with the humanitarian sentiment.

To this Demon of the Absolute, expressing itself in a meaningless fixity or in an equally meaningless flux, Dr. More declared himself unalterably opposed, preferring the inexplicable dogma of the combined humanity and divinity of Christ.

Transferring his analysis to literature, Dr. More discovered a similar dichotomy, represented by the neo-classicists on the one hand, with their "rules" and "unities," and the modernists on the other, with their denial of all authority and their enthronement of personal whim.

In science as well Dr. More finds the Demon of the Absolute at work setting up a mechanical behaviorism in opposition to the former subjective psychology.

But while in no field is there an absolute and fixed standard, still human experience has proved the comparatively universal validity of certain ideas and works of genius. In literature for instance, lines from the Greek Anthology, Jonson's verses to Celia, and Goethe's "Wanderers Nachtlied" are universal in their sentiment and speak direct to human nature, in Japan as well as in the west.

In conclusion, Dr. More declared war again on the Demon of the Absolute, but especially on the naturalists, who proclaim the absolutism of the eternal flux and of personal whim.

A touch of humor was added to the address when Dr. More referred to himself as the least read and the most hated critic of our day. That his position is predominantly conservative can not account for this neglect. Perhaps the reason is that Dr. More, instead of rejoicing in that varying proportion of sanity which is to be found in all men, has an uncanny faculty of quoting the extreme and unguarded statements of his opponents and belaboring them, as if these were all. In the ensuing warfare, Mr. More's head is bloody, but unbowed.

Still one wonders if there is not some more genial way of holding the golden mean and of rediscovering the divinity which Christ proved was in mankind.

The modesty of Oberlin College in making the goal of the campaign only four million and a half dollars is attested by the fact that Ohio Wesleyan is in the midst of a campaign for eight million dollars, while Western Reserve University is reported to be on the eve of a campaign for twenty million dollars. Judge King of Sandusky at the campaign conference stated that within the next five years Ohio State University is contemplating adding thirty million dollars to her resources. In our own field Oberlin is not accustomed to playing second fiddle to these friendly rivals of ours. If Ohio Wesleyan can and will raise eight million dollars — well, the rest need not be said.

ESSAY PRIZE

Due to the fact that there was almost no competition the prizes totaling $100 offered for the best essay on a literary critical subject were not given this spring. Instead the date of the closing of the contest has been postponed until January 10, 1924.

The Baccalaureate Sermon

President Henry C. King, '79

We cannot well ignore the fact that we are today in the midst of the celebration of the ninetieth anniversary of Oberlin College and Community. Any Christian college, if it is true to its calling, is a kind of type of the whole kingdom of God, of which it is a part. Its growth is a representation in miniature of the development of that whole kingdom of God. We may see, therefore, the fundamental laws of the growing temple of God illustrated in the growth of Oberlin College, and especially in the personal factors of the ninety years of the life of Oberlin, individual and social. I am thus taking as my text the great all-embracing promise of Christ to the Church at Philadelphia. As Charles says: "From the words of our author it is clear that its Christianity was of a high character, standing in point of merit second only to Smyrna among the seven Churches. In the time of Ignatius it enjoyed the same high reputation. . . . In later times Philadelphia was notable for the heroism with which it resisted the growing power of the Turks." In Ramsay's words, "It displayed all the noble qualities of endurance, truth and steadfastness which are attributed to it in the letter of St. John, amid the ever threatening danger of Turkish attack; and its story rouses even Gibbon to admiration." It is not too much to say that qualities like these have repeatedly marked the history of Oberlin. And this is the promise to such qualities which I am making my text: "He that overcometh, I will make him a pillar in the temple of my God, and he shall go out thence no more: and I will write upon him the name of my God, and the name of the city of my God, the new Jerusalem, which cometh down out of heaven from my God, and mine own new name."

Here are suggested at once both the fields and the rewards of spiritual victory: first, in the figure of the pillar in the temple; second, in the more explicit assurance of a threefold fellowship: with God,—"the name of the city of my God"; and sharing in the new and victorious revelation of God in Christ,—"mine own new name."

And first, let us remind ourselves of the sweep of the first promise to the overcomer: "I will make him a pillar in the temple of my God, and he shall go out thence no more."

This is the thrilling assurance that a man's life need not be meaningless, but may be builded permanently into the growing temple of God; that he may help forever in its support and development; that he may have an everlasting share and a place of honor in the kingdom of the Spirit; that it is in the heart of God to put every one of his overcoming children into the place fittest for him, the place best for his precise qualities, the place chosen by the Divine Architect, the place of a glorious pillar in the temple of God and of humanity. His victory is achieved. "He shall go out thence no more."

Forty years ago, at the fiftieth anniversary of the College, President Fairchild preached upon "Providential Aspects of the Oberlin Enterprise," from the text, "Except the Lord build the house they labor in vain that build it." His entire sermon might be said to be illustrations of the promise of our text,—of how life after life, group after group, circumstance after circumstance, favorable and unfavorable, under the Divine Architect were builded into a worthy and noble embodiment of the spirit of the kingdom of God. Let one illustration suffice: "When Mr. Shipherd started from Elyria on horseback, with three dollars in his pocket and the burden of a great work upon his heart, confidently expecting colonists and students and teachers to join him in his enterprise, and bring a community and a college into existence in the forest in the space of a few months, it was not merely his own judgment and reason that sustained him. He believed that the Lord had given him a charge, and that he was to go on his way doubting nothing."

In the fifty years covered by President Fairchild's survey fell the brief but unique achievement of the two founders, Shipherd and Stewart; the rugged supporting strength of the early colonists illustrated in the first pioneer, Peter Pease; the three vigorous presidencies of Mahan and of Finney, and in chief part, of Fairchild himself; the service as Trustees of such broad-visioned men as Father Keep and Michael D. Strieby; the inspiration as teachers of such men as Morgan and Dascomb and Monroe.

Here are a group of powerful personalities

of very varied kinds, who would have been notable anywhere, but who so built their lives into the work of this College as both to make a lasting contribution to its life, and to leave an enduring memory in the minds of hundreds of students. It may be doubted if they could have counted more anywhere else. A similar thing could be said of other groups in the later college generations, like Ellis and Churchill and Shurtleff and Judson Smith and Mrs. Johnston. Strong personalities have not ceased, as the notable work of Professor Anderegg and Dr. Leonard—the latest called home—bears convincing testimony. These all have been made pillars in the growing temple of the College and of the kingdom of God.

But the final temple of God is no mere human structure, however stupendous and glorious. Later in his book the Seer of Revelation writes of the New Jerusalem: " I saw no temple therein: for the Lord God the Almighty, and the Lamb, are the temple thereof." That is, the ultimate reality for men in the realm of the Spirit is not instrumentalities of any kind, however great and sacred, but an ever-growing sharing in the eternal realities of the life of God himself.

Our text therefore goes on to put the great promise to the overcomer in all-embracing personal terms: " I will write upon him the name of my God and the name of the city of my God, and mine own new name." These are no external marks. The name stands for the person. To write thus upon a man means that he belongs to God, that he belongs to the fellowship of the city of God, that he belongs to Christ,—to the fellowship of the supreme revelation of God in Christ.

In the first place, *to write upon a man "the name of my God"* carries with it the revelation of the creative will of God in men's *common* nature. It involves the great supreme common values, that make a man a man: the gift of a nature like God's, of a spiritual life like God's, the gift of personality, of thought, of feeling, of will; the possibility of sharing in the eternal values of Truth, Goodness and Beauty; the power to share personally in the life of God and in all his eternal purposes. This is to say that man is in very truth made in the image of God,—a child of God. Any religion worthy the name must root in such a conception of the fundamental creation of men in the image of God. Any other view essentially belittles man.

This basically religious view of men—that feels that men and God are inextricably akin —has characterized Oberlin College from its first beginning. John Frederic Oberlin, whose name was deliberately chosen to characterize the whole enterprise, was both a profoundly gifted and profoundly religious man. The Oberlin Covenant grew out of the purpose of Founders and Colonists alike to dedicate both Colony and College, with all their individual members, to the service of God. The missionary impulse sprang inevitably out of such a purpose. Nor was it an accident that equal educational privileges were given to women, and that race barriers were broken down, and anti-slavery principles adopted. These were all part and parcel of the absolute conviction that every human being was made in the image of God, and that wrong to any man was a defiance of the Infinite Father.

First of all, then, must it be said, to him that overcometh: " I will write upon him the name of my God," for he belongs to God, and is bound to him by every fibre of his being.

In the second place, Christ promises to the overcomer: "*I will write upon him the name of the city of my God.*" The individual nature of man must fruit inevitably in a worthy conception of the society of humanity,—" the city of my God, the new Jerusalem, which cometh down out of heaven from my God." This is the embodied ideal and purpose of God for human society,—a civilization that shall be permeated through and through with the standards and ideals of Christ. Now, the civilization of Christ's own choice—the civilization of brotherly men, of triumphant love—can only be achieved in the measure in which the building of personal lives into institutions goes steadily forward, bringing into all organizations and groups of men the same principles and ideals as hold for individuals.

No lesson of the war was clearer than this. And Charles—the latest and ablest of commentators on Revelation—believes that this is the great outstanding teaching of that book: " John the Seer insists not only that the individual follower of Christ should fashion his principles and conduct by the teaching of Christ, but that all governments should model their policies by the same Christian norm. He proclaims that there can be no divergence between the moral laws binding on the individual and those incumbent on the State, or any voluntary society or corporation within the State.

None can be exempt from these obligations.

Fellowship comes by fellowship. It can come in no other way. The world's life today is too complexly interrelated, too much a solidarity to escape the demands of coöperation and fellowship. We know that it is impossible to live an isolated life in commerce, in industry, in science, in art, in literature; and it is futile folly to suppose that we can achieve such isolation in political and international relations. We must come into the fellowship of the nations. We must take our fair share of world responsibility under honorable conditions which we can determine. Our own self-respect, our own growth, our own character and influence and happiness require the international task, and hence the international mind —world fellowship.

Even the church of Christ must see clearly that the vital parts of its life are not machinery and organization, as Fairbairn says, but its Christlike persons. " The Church is a large term; it does not denote Churches; polity is not of its essence, saints and souls are. The priest and the presbyter, the bishop and the preacher, are of the accidents of the Churches, not of the essence of the Church; the sainted father or mother, the holy home, the godly man, the living Spirit, are of the essence of the Church, not of the accidents of the Church. And it is through what is of the essence of the Church that the authority of God is manifested and His truth apprehended. It is holiness that creates holiness, God in the priest or preacher or parent that creates godliness and obedience in the soul. . . . Now, it is remarkable that in the language of Christ as to the kingdom the emphasis falls, not upon the officials, if officials there be, or on Sacramental acts, if such acts there be, but upon the people, upon persons, their personal qualities, conduct, character, their state and living before God, their behaviour and ministry among men."

Precisely the same thing is to be said of the Christian college. Its mechanisms and abundance of things—imperative as they are—are of the accidents of the college. The priceless personal lives builded into it, and incarnating the intellectual and spiritual ideals of the race, —these are of the essence of the college.

All values go back finally to the riches of personal lives. And the best test of education is the significance of the persons it sends forth. I am thinking, therefore, especially just now of the long roll of the alumni and former students of the college; for they show what the college is and what it has done as does nothing else.

In the questionnaire sent out this year to all the former students of the College was a question asking a report upon any special honors conferred. One answer to that question I may fitly quote here, not primarily for its own beauty, but because it seems to me so typical of a great army of the unsung who are

> " . . . finding amplest recompense
> For life's ungarlanded expense
> In work done squarely and un-
>   wasted days."

—because, that is, it was such an answer as might have been honestly made by many another in Oberlin's long roll of graduates and former students:

It must be that there are many graduates who feel reluctant, as I do, to record themselves as worthy of honorable mention, who are just fathers or mothers, and yet who like to believe they have counted in the life of their time and of their community somewhat beyond the rays of the library lamp. We have pushed here and pulled there, with no vague sense of loyalty to the standards we have come to call " the Oberlin ideals." We see life, it sometimes appears, differently. That bit of vision, that willingness, now and then, to " trust the soul's invincible surmise," we cannot doubt, has revealed itself in our ways of life.

So, for myself, I cannot muster the courage to set down, concretely, as achievements or honors, some activities that have flowered inevitably from the seedtime at Oberlin. It may be that, in your report, you will want to mention, in some fashion, these unknown soldiers among us. We have tried to be good citizens, good parents, good Christians. The obligations of our personal lives have pressed hard. Through them and beyond them, we have unflaggingly pursued the vision of something greater than ourselves.

These are some of the questions that have interested me, for example, for which, I have talked in schools, clubs, granges, movie-theatres, written in our little country papers and tried to further with what leisure and energy I could spare: library extension; books for children; musical education; choosing pictures for our homes; suffrage; prohibition; good government; civic obligations; the religious life. During the war I served in various executive ways and was called upon to give my services as a speaker on patriotic subjects.

My experience must be that of many who cannot specify to what titles they may aspire, who are just thankful for the young lives developing about them. These may do some of the great and fine things we have willed and hoped to see.

I like to say over the lovely phrases of Robert Louis Stevenson, in his Triplex. They sum up the Oberlin tradition: " Every heart that has beat strong and cheerfully has left a hopeful impulse behind it in the world, and bettered the tradition of mankind."

I congratulate the living Oberlin men and women that they belong to a fellowship, of whom a letter like that can be honestly written—a fellowship of "the city of God."

But there is a third promise of Christ to him that overcometh: " I will write upon him mine own new name." God reveals himself to men chiefly, not only in the expression of his creative will in the common personal and social nature of men, but also in their own unique individuality, and in the supreme manifestation of himself in Christ.

A " new name " is indicative of passing into a new life, a new purpose, a new character. So elsewhere Christ promises the overcomer: " I will give him a white stone and upon the stone a new name written, which none knoweth but him that receiveth it." The new name is a secret between the man and God. No other can fully know it. He is called of God to the peculiar task that the new name foreshadows, to his special message and mission. The new name stands for that secret word which God gives him, and which in turn he must manifest in some fashion to other men. It stands for the giving to others of the miracle of his own unique individuality, which is truly his own and which no man can take from him. This it is which makes the richness and the unceasing interest of the growing temple of God.

And in the end a man's deepest message and service to others must go back to God's completest revelation of himself to the man,—to the supreme manifestation in Christ, as that gradually comes home to him,—Christ's own new name written upon him. God is thus giving himself to us as he asks that we should give ourselves to him—a unique gift on both sides. All for God, and God for all. For each has his own possibility of unique reflection of the infinite life of God.

We do not speak, then, with strict accuracy when we talk of filling another man's place. The College never filled the places of Maban and Finney and Fairchild; or of Ballantine and Barrows; or of any one of the rich roll of

its teachers. We shall not fill the places of Professor Anderegg and Dr. Leonard. Each man is an ever-living stone filling his own unique place in the eternally growing kingdom of God. And all the varied personalities, who have been builded into Oberlin College, have helped to enrich its life and under God have done an inviolate and sacred work. The man who follows another cannot, then, replace him. But both men, if they are utterly true, each to the self with which God endowed him, may be enduring pillars in the temple of God.

It is of wealth of persons, then, that we chiefly think today—the spirit that prompted the lavish giving of " the alabaster cruise of exceeding precious ointment ": the sacrifices of unnamed women and children in the families of the early pioneers and in days of difficulty since; the willingness of both gifted and humble men and women to stand for great forward movements against persistent misinterpretation and bitter opposition; generous givers of their means and of their personalities as well, like the Tappans, the Warners, the Severances, and Hall; givers of stimulating ideas like Theodore Weld and William Cochran and Finney and Fairchild; promoters of the world of the beautiful in music and art like Allen and Rice and Mrs. Johnston; exemplars of the scientific spirit like the Wrights; distinguished public servants like Cox and Monroe and Burton; the great list of those whose work is shadowed forth in Oberlin's "History of Honor"; unusual classes like '75 and '85; and men and women—how many of them—who in their student days helped to make the college life a finer, stronger, broader thing.

Members of the Graduating Classes:

You stand in the line of a great and rich personal heritage. Unnumbered lives out of all the ninety years of the work of the College have ministered to you. You come into a fellowship of college alumni in which you may take just pride, and to whose significance you are to add. You have faced in your college course the best the race has had to give you.

You are called to be, therefore, of those who by the grace of God overcome, who are to be pillars in the temple of God, upon whom shall be written the name of God, the name of the city of God, and Christ's own new name. So supreme is your calling!

That calling means, first, that you are in.

(Concluded on next page, second column)

Honorary Degrees

Candidates for honorary degrees were presented by Professor A. S. Root. Due to lack of space only the characterizations spoken by President King while conferring the degrees are here recorded.

DOCTOR OF LAWS

NEWTON DIEHL BAKER, Attorney-at-Law, former Secretary of War, Cleveland, Ohio: "broad and thoughtful student of public questions, rarely gifted public teacher, distinguished public servant in circumstances of peculiar difficulty."

PAUL DRENNAN CRAVATH, Attorney-at-Law, New York, N. Y.: "lawyer of extraordinary ability, an ability put unstintedly at the service of his country when service of the highest order was dequired."

ROBERT ERNEST VINSON, President of Western Reserve University, Cleveland, Ohio: "able scholar, teacher and administrator, interpreter to his generation of great intellectual and spiritual values."

DOCTOR OF DIVINITY

ERNEST BOURNER ALLEN, Pastor of the Pilgrim Congregational Church of Oak Park, Ill.: "devoted and broad-visioned minister to the spiritual needs of men, a Christian statesman."

EVAN WALTER SCOTT, Chief of Chaplains of the United States Navy, Washington, D. C.: "honored leader in an honored service."

DOCTOR OF LETTERS

EDWARD CAPPS, Professor of Classics in Princeton University, Princeton, N. J.: "distinguished scholar, author, and editor, effective witness to the permanent values of the classical world."

DOCTOR OF SCIENCE

CHARLES JOSEPH CHAMBERLAIN, Professor of Morphology and Cytology in the University of Chicago, Chicago, Ill.: "thorough scholar, scientific investigator, and world-traveler, steadily extending the bounds of human knowledge in the realm of Botany."

HENRY GRANDLER COWLES, Professor of Plant Ecology in the University of Chicago, Chicago, Ill.: "honored pioneer, leader, and teacher in the field of plant ecology."

MASTER OF ARTS

ARCHER HAYES SHAW, Member of the editorial staff of the Cleveland *Plain Dealer*, Cleveland, Ohio: "wholesome and potent factor through many years in the press of a great city."

JOHN MACALPINE SIDDALL, Editor-in-Chief of the *American Magazine*, New York, N. Y.: "acute observer of his time, faithful steward of a great human trust, and inspirer of common men."

AMOS ALONZO STAGG, Director of the Department of Physical Culture and Athletics in the University of Chicago, Chicago, Ill.: "a recognized leader in the field of physical education, and standing for the highest ideals of sportsmanship in college athletics."

The Baccalaureate Sermon

(Concluded)

alienably akin to God, and by that very kinship you belong to God. You are called to work triumphantly in the line of his mighty will.

It means, second, that you are made on so large a plan that you cannot come to your best independent of one another. You are made for fellowship, not for isolation. You are members one of another. You belong, therefore, to the City of God. You are called to a world-fellowship.

It means, third, that you are divinely endowed with a unique individuality with its own unique reflection of the revelation of God in Christ. You are to be absolutely true to your own best vision. You belong to the truest and highest you know. To the embodiment of this, you are called.

May the great promises to the overcomer be fulfilled for you all: "He that overcometh, I will make him a pillar in the temple of my God, and he shall go out hence no more: and I will write upon him the name of my God, and the name of the city of my God. and mine own new name."

The Trustee Meeting

The Semi-Annual Meeting of the Board of Trustees of Oberlin College was held in the Administration Building, Monday, June 18, 1923, beginning at 9:30 o'clock.

DR. WARNER'S GOLDEN ANNIVERSARY

At the opening of the trustee meeting President King presented to Dr. Lucien C. Warner a gold medallion in commemoration of the completion of fifty years of service on the Board of Trustees. The medallion has on one side

CHESTER C. HARBISON
Appointed **Professor of Public Speaking**

the seal of the college and on the other the following inscription: "Lucien C. Warner, In commemoration of fifty years of service on the Board of Trustees of Oberlin College, 'datio dei permanent justis.'"

309 DEGREES APPROVED

The trustees voted to approve the recommendation of the faculty for the granting of degrees and diplomas to members of this year's class at the graduation exercises of Wednesday, June 20, as follows: Bachelor of Arts, 258; Master of Arts, 11; Bachelor of Music, 21; Bachelor of School Music, 9; Bachelor of Divinity, 10; total, 309.

A BUDGET OF $783,000

The budget for the year 1923-24, as adopted by the trustees at this meeting, carries appropriations amounting to $783,000. Of this amount $400,500 will be provided by semester bills of students, and the remainder from the income from the endowment and other funds of the college, and by gifts to be solicited from the friends of the college for the purpose.

DEAN BOSWORTH RESIGNS

The trustees accepted the resignation of Dr. Edward I. Bosworth as Dean of the Graduate School of Theology. Dr. Bosworth continues his work as Professor of the New Testament Language and Literature in the School of Theology. In his place as Dean the trustees appointed Dr. Thomas W. Graham, Professor of Homiletics in the School of Theology.

FACULTY CHANGES

Professor Howard H. Carter was appointed Professor Emeritus after forty-two years of service as teacher of pianoforte in the Conservatory of Music.

The trustees granted leave of absence for the coming year, as follows: Louis E. Lord, Professor of the Latin Language and Literature, for study and travel; Robert A. Budington, Professor of Zoölogy, for study and travel; Herbert Harroun, Professor of Singing, for study and travel; George W. Andrews, Professor of Organ and Composition, for travel, during the first semester of the coming year; Wilbert L. Carr, Assistant Professor of Latin, for one semester, for special research under the direction of the Classical League of America; Miss Florence L. Joy, Instructor in English, for further study.

NEW APPOINTMENTS

To fill the vacancy caused by the death of Dr. Fred E. Leonard, the trustees appointed Dr. Whitelaw R. Morrison as Professor of Hygiene and Physical Education and Director of the Men's Gymnasium. Dr. Morrison graduated from Oberlin College in the class of 1910 and from the medical school of Columbia University in 1914. Since 1917 he has been at the University of Cincinnati as head of the department of physical education.

Chester Clyde Harbison was appointed Professor of Public speaking. He comes to Oberlin after very successful teaching in Fairmount College, Wichita, Kansas.

(Concluded on page 18, col. 2)

Theological Commencement

Kemper Fullerton

With the commencement exercises of May 20-23 the Oberlin Graduate School of Theology closed its ninetieth year of service and girded up its loins for the last decade in a century of honest endeavor in the cause of the Kingdom of God. Unmolested by theological controversy, unembittered by the passions and intrigues which heresy trials always engender, united in spirit but with just enough difference in intellectual outlook to provide the necessary stimulus for the mental life of the student body, the Faculty of Oberlin have been able to teach the truth as they saw it constructively and not polemically. The spirit of contentiousness has never been given opportunity to bite or devour among us. As a result this School of Theology has been privileged to attempt the reinterpretation of the Gospel message in the light of the new conditions in the modern world of thought without the friction and spiritual waste which so often accompanies intellectual change, and its students have been accustomed to breathe an air of serenity. As one who came to Oberlin from the outside and from a torrid zone of theological controversy, the writer may be allowed thus to express what has always seemed to him to be the outstanding characteristic of Oberlin. Few institutions can boast an intellectual and spiritual climate more bland and equable.

Through the quiet communion service on the afternoon of Baccalaureate Sunday, with which the various exercises of commencement week began, the spirit of our school found fitting expression. Mr. Graham, who has done so much during the last two years to make good the loss sustained by college and community through the departure of Mr. Hutchins to Berea, gave the baccalaureate sermon with his accustomed earnestness and vigor. His theme, *Faith*, could not have been more aptly chosen for times like these. The Commencement address was delivered by Rev. Lynn Harold Hough of Detroit. He discussed in a stimulating way *The Mind of the Preacher* and outlined the various intellectual obligations 'which rest upon him. Dr. Hough sounded a note not often heard and sorely needed at a time when there is often more reliance upon organization than upon ideas. The Conservatory, as usual, generously contributed to the attractiveness of our commencement programmes. Oberlin is indeed fortunate in always having its academic exercises wreathed about with pleasant harmonies.

The Alumni Supper, the name of which, by the way, the Faculty wish was more amply justified by a larger number of returning sons, is usually one of the most enjoyable features in the calendar of our Oberlin life. This year proved no exception. Under the leadership of Mr. Fiske as toastmaster, we were treated to one of the best series of after dinner speeches we have had in years. The catholicity of Oberlin was reflected in the speakers and the speeches. Dr. Hough, for the Methodists, told us how greatly he was indebted to Congregational theologians. Dr. Ernest Bourner Allen, class of 1903, congratulated Dr. Hough on his discriminating taste in theological diet. Mr. Bedros Apelian, class of 1913, in a very happy speech, represented our contribution to the Presbyterians. Mr. Lyman Cady of the class of 1916 and of the Shantung Christian College, was an evidence of what we are trying to do for the cause of Christian Unity. His clear-cut and admirable analysis of the problems confronting missions in China will not soon be forgotten. Our own Mr. Hannah is an ever-ready and convincing witness to the wit and learning we have drawn from the Church of England, while Mr. Randall not only represented the Senior Class but the Disciples as well.

In the daily grind of seeding-time during the school year we are now and again in danger of losing sight of the meaning of our work. The trivial round, the common task fails, it may be, to connect itself very obviously with the larger whole of a subject or with the life of the institution. But in the flowering-time of the commencement season the final meaning of all that has preceded discloses itself and we all thank God and take courage for another year.

The Trustee Meeting
(Concluded from page 17)

Other new appointments approved by the trustees included the following: Miss Blanche Lindsay, Instructor in Zoölogy; Miss Margaret R. Schauffler, Instructor in Fine Arts; Leslie H. Jolliff, Instructor in Organ and Pianoforte; Miss Marion Shaw, Head Cataloguer in the College Library.

College Work in Shansi

Wynn C. Fairfield, '07

The college department of the Oberlin schools in Shansi is gradually being differentiated from the rest of the school, but is still at the stage where it counts for less in school life than the high school department which has held the center of the stage for so many years. The enrolment for the year was twenty-seven, of whom fourteen are in the graduating class. Most of these fourteen are graduates either from our own high school in previous years or from the sister high school in Fenchow, the other American Board mission station in Shansi, but a few are from government schools. Ten out of the class have had from one to six years of experience as teachers in primary schools or as preachers, and are more mature therefore than Freshmen and Sophomores are apt to be. It has been hard for some of them to readjust themselves to the necessary limitations of school life again after the years of. more or less independent existence. Because of this delay in continuing their studies, the class as a whole had not had as good a training in English and some other subjects as our present high school graduates, and a large share of our effort has been directed toward giving them a working knowledge of English so that they will be prepared to use it in university work, which is largely carried on in English.

Two years of work are offered, making the equivalent of the junior college or Freshman and Sophomore years. Upon graduation they can enter the senior college of Shantung Christian University in the arts course, or the second year of the senior college in Peking University, which has changed to the new educational system. A number of our graduates have preferred to enter government universities. This year, eleven of the college graduates are in senior colleges, seven are teaching, three are preaching, and one is doing secretarial work. There have been twenty-three graduates in all in the five graduating classes.

The number of years of college work to be offered has been a vexed and is still a vexing question. As originally projected, the course covered four years, with a curriculum similar to that of an American college of the Oberlin type. But changes in the Chinese government curriculum, which had been based on the Japanese educational system, led to a change in our own work and the first class graduated from a junior college with three years of work. Further readjustments of the government system led to a shortening of our college work to two years, the standard length for a junior college course to be followed by four years of university work. Now leading Chinese educators have voted in favor of a remodeling of the whole educational system, and and an edict has been issued authorizing the change to six years primary, six years of high school and four years of university or college work. As this gives one more year before college than the former system, our present college is cut in two, and we shall have to add an extra year to maintain its status as a junior college, so returning to the number of years of study of the first class.

This junior college should increasingly provide for vocational training for the high school graduates who are financially able to take a general high school course and a couple of years beyond it, but are not able to bear the expense of a full university course. The number of mission and government high schools is steadily growing, and more and more students of limited financial ability are graduating, many of whom will not be able to stand the expense of a trip to Peking or Shantung Christian Universities in addition to the cost of an education there. The round trip to Peking now costs two-thirds as much as a year's board in our college, and the round trip to Tsinanfu, the site of Shantung Christian University, a good deal more than a year's board here. If adequate financial support is assured, a full college on a coeducational basis would serve an increasing constituency not only in Shansi but in the provinces to the west as well, as one of the main lines of east and west travel passes through central Shansi. Such a college would realize the dream of the first group of Oberlin students who more than forty years ago came out to China fired with the vision of reproducing in China a school with the spirit of their Alma Mater.

Professor Lynds Jones, with a class of seventeen students, left June 21 for the annual ecology trip to the Pacific coast.

Laura Shurtleff Price, '93

Harriet E. Penfield, '98

How fortunately gifted are those who have a warm outgoing friendliness, an unassuming sincerity, who are always interested in people, and who respond to a wide range of types. All who know Laura Shurtleff Price would agree that she is one of those whose life is so expressed in terms of human relationships rather than in terms of things. And her closer friends know her as a friend absolutely dependable in every relation,—for friendship is the very keynote of her life.

With a sympathetic heart and a keen, analytical mind, her character presents many contrasts, sensitiveness and delicacy of feeling combined with clear-cut decision and matter-of-fact common sense. The light touch of humor is hers also. There is much of the literary artist's keen sense in her quick and humorous characterizations of people and situations.

In action she is practical and energetic. She can get things done. She plans carefully and then works persistently until the undertaking is accomplished, be it large or small. She has little patience with that enthusiasm which overlooks systematic detail.

No wonder that Laura Price is much in demand for executive and committee work,—in South Chicago settlement work, in the old Association of Collegiate Alumnae, in the Parent-Teacher Association, in various campaigns to give Chicago a better city government, in the Vocational Scholarship League, and in countless Oberlin affairs.

In all these she has given herself unstintingly, as she always does, sometimes completing the work through sheer grit, for she is not always equal physically to the task she sets herself. But she does complete it, with the same spirit of loyalty that she shows in her friendships.

Laura Shurtleff was born in Oberlin. Her father, General Giles W. Shurtleff, a graduate of the college, was connected with it for many years. Her mother graduated from Painesville Seminary. Mrs. Price's uncle, ex-Senator Theodore E. Burton, one of Oberlin's Alumni Trustees and now for many years a national figure, was often in their home during Laura's girlhood. Rather surprising it is, that to her uncle, economist and statesman, she credits much of her love of poetry, as she traces her love of general literature to her father.

After her graduation, Laura Shurtleff taught for a few years in smaller places and then made up her mind she would like best to teach in Chicago. With characteristic energy she accomplished her desire and had several years of interesting teaching in the South Division High School.

In 1903 she married Samuel Harrison Price, who died in 1918. Mr. Price was of English descent and had many of the best traits of an English country gentleman of the 19th century along with those of an up-to-date Chicagoan. Laura Price and her husband had many similar tastes. They both loved the out-of-doors, and loved to motor about the country and take their friends. Their home was a place of delightful hospitality. Truly, the genius for friendship belonged to them both!

Laura Price's interest in Oberlin finds expression in various ways, but in none, I think, more effectively than in the Oberlin Women's Club of Chicago. Oberlin women had not been organized in Chicago, except at one time L. L. S. and Aelioian groups. Another group met for luncheon for some years but informally, with no organization. In large measure the credit belongs to Laura Price for starting an organization of all Oberlin women in Chicago and its schools, and making it a going con-

(Concluded on page 22)

Paul Drennan Cravath, '82, LL.D., '23

Herbert A. Miller

Both parents of Paul Drennan Cravath of the class of 1882 were born the year of the founding of Oberlin College. Both were members of the class of 1857. His mother, "a demure Quaker girl," resented the custom by which a member of the faculty read the graduating es-.

After graduating from Oberlin Paul Cravath went to Columbia Law School, in which he made an exceptionally brilliant record, winning the prize tutorship in law, and on graduation entering at once one of the best law firms of New York. His legal career began just at the time

PAUL DRENNAN CRAVATH, '82, LL.D. '23

says of the girls, and she protested and won for women the privilege of reading for themselves. His father came to Oberlin intending to become a lawyer, but the Oberlin influence turned him to the ministry. Paul was born in Berlin Heights, where his father held his first and only pastorate, going from there to the war as chaplain and then into missionary educational work. While in Europe with the Fisk Jubilee Singers Mr. Cravath put his son in charge of a French professor for two years of his preparatory work. The knowledge of

French then secured stood him in good stead later, when trusts and corporations were beginning to supplant the old methods of finance and industry, and he became one of the most important factors in the constructive organization of national and international organizations of this sort. He has been from the beginning one of the leading corporation lawyers in America.

In addition to his active professional life he has taken a vital interest in social, civic, and political affairs. He married Agnes Huntington, who had achieved great success as a singer, and he has always been a leading supporter of the opera and other artistic interests in New York. He was for many years chairman of the New York Tenement House Commission, and has been on many local committees of that sort. He was a member of the mission representing the United States treasury to the Inter-Allied War Conference in Paris, and advisory counsel of the American Mission to the Inter-Allied Council on War Purchases and Finance, London and Paris. General Pershing gave him the Distinguished Service Medal for "exceptionally meritorious conduct and services during the war." He was made a Chevalier of the Legion of Honor in France and an honorary Bencher of Gray's Inn, London. (The accompanying photograph was taken from the portrait which hangs in Gray's Inn.)

Mr. Cravath is president of the Italy-America Society, and during the spring spent a month in Rome. On June 28, at a luncheon on board the Conte Verde, the latest addition to Italian merchant-marine, according to the New York *Times:*

"The Ambassador, on behalf of the King of Italy, conferred upon Mr. Cravath the Medal of a Commendatore di S. S. Maurizio e Lazaro in recognition of his 'sincere friendship for Italy,' and his efforts to bring about a closer understanding between the two peoples. He congratulated the company on the inauguration of another steamer of the first-class giving direct service to Italian ports, and said that service of this kind would bring the countries closer together."

He has taken up the mantle of his father, who was the founder and first president of Fisk University, by becoming chairman of the board of trustees of that institution.

Physically Mr. Cravath is impressive, standing six feet four inches and well proportioned. He has one daughter, Mrs. James Larkin of New York, who came to commencement with him. His only sister is Mrs. H. A. Miller of Oberlin.

CONSERVATORY COMMENCEMENT

The two parts of the Conservatory Commencement in which the twenty-one graduates took part, assisted by members of the faculty and the orchestra, maintained the usual high standards of the Conservatory graduation exercises.

DR. HELEN F. COCHRAN

Dr. Helen Finney Cochran, director of the Women's Gymnasium and professor of hygiene and physical education, died in Cincinnati on Monday afternoon, July 2d, as a result of an operation for appendicitis. The funeral services were held at the home of her father, Wm. C. Cochran, '69, on Wednesday morning, July 4th.

The sudden death of Dr. Cochran comes as a great shock to her many friends and is undoubtedly a serious loss for the department of Physical Education.

The news comes too late for the Alumni Magazine to do more than make this brief note and express to her family the universal sympathy of all Oberlin alumni.

Laura Shurtleff Price

(Concluded from page 20)

cern with definite purposes and a source of much enjoyment as well. She was its first president, but it is as secretary that her continuous work has been done. Keeping up a list of names may sound prosaic, but it is no light task in a great city, where people come and go and every moving day changes addresses. If she does not know that a person lives at the address given she will sooner or later actually go to the address and find out. Many an Oberlinite has first found her way to a meeting of the club because Mrs. Price has invited her. She has an ambition to keep up this method. She says she never expected to be a candidate for office, but that she is out for election as secretary of the Oberlin Woman's Club of Chicago.

In the great Oberlin campaign Mrs. Price is chairman of the woman's division for Chicago, one of the most important positions in the organization. One thing is certain: whatever can be done, that Mrs. Price will do.

The Secret of Musical Performance

Edward Dickinson

One who devotes his life to a search for the secret of music finds that there is no end to learning. It is conceivable that one may at last know everything that is to be known about musical science. but the *spirit* of music is more wonderful and evasive the longer one strives to delve into its meaning. Every new experience is a new revelation. The marvelous power of music over the human heart has never been explained. One who seeks it is like the man who sought for the mystic tem-

ple in the enchanted forest; he heard the ringing of its bells, now full, now faint—the temple he could not find. It is of course the mystery of all art, of every manifestation of beauty. "Technique," said Ruskin, "is only skill; art is mystery and spiritual power." And its spiritual power is so great just because its mystery is so deep. The two terms are involved in one another, for there can be no spiritual power where there is no mystery. If religion could be freed from mystery, and faith become sight, there would no longer be religion.

In the performance of music the problem is that of technique vs. expression,—it is the problem of the performer, the listener, and the critic. It is supremely the problem of the teacher. Technique can be taught; can expression also be taught? Why does one player charm and move us, while another of equal or perhaps superior technical skill moves us not at all? Can the supreme quality without which technical skill is of little worth, be taught by formal method or aroused by means of example?

This old question has been much in my mind while listening to the performance of advanced Conservatory students during the past few months. What one notices most in the playing and singing of young musicians is a lack of individuality. Some listeners call it a lack of feeling, but it is not a lack of feeling. It is rather a lack of that form of imaginative power which enables the performer to enter into the mood of the composer and interpret it in terms of the performer's own musical experience and musical passion. This is a somewhat enigmatical saying, but every musician knows what is meant by it. It is the expression of one's own personality through the medium of another's creation. The problem is the same in acting. There are as many Hamlets as there are actors who play the part. There are as many *Chromatic Fantasies* as there are pianists who play it. Says Oscar Wilde: "When Rubinstein plays to us the *Sonata Appassionata* of Beethoven, he gives us not merely Beethoven, but also himself, and so gives us Beethoven absolutely—Beethoven reinterpreted through a rich artistic nature. and made vivid and wonderful to us by a new and intense, personality." Arthur Symons writing of Ysaye's playing in the *Kreutzer Sonata*, says: "In that instant a beauty which had never been in the world came into the world. That thing was neither Beethoven nor Ysaye, it was made out of their meeting, and just that miracle could never occur again."

The playing of such men as Rubinstein and Ysaye presupposes consummate technique, but it is more than technique; it is technique illuminated by something more than technical aptitude or labor or knowledge can give. It is not feeling alone, for it is a power of which the possessor is largely unconscious. The nearest word for it is personality—personality manifesting itself by means of tones. It is a part of the "mystery" of which Ruskin speaks. Without some measure of this power to carry over a rich, vibrant personality to the hearer a musical performance, however skillful, cannot move or charm the hearer,—it can only excite or astonish him

Most young people lack this quality. Yet all have the germs of it,—can it be increased and made operative in their music? An English philosopher, Henry Sturt, has this shrewd observation: "I once read an absurd remark that the piano-playing of a young girl full of feeling is more artistically satisfying than that of a more skillful middle-aged performer. This is the Byronic fallacy. The playing of young people is generally cold. They are full of feeling, but it is feeling about themselves, the sort that has no immediate value for art."

The young person, therefore, must develop the feeling that has " immediate value for art." He must remember that expression in playing is not following certain rules, but is self-expression. There must be something in the soul to express. It is the problem of the making of a full, vivid personality. There are many ways; three at least are imperative,— there must be enthusiasm, musical culture, and general culture. In those admirable books edited by James Francis Cooke, in which famous pianists and singers discourse on their art, I have been struck with the persistence with which they insist that the student should give constant study to literature, art, history, and other agencies of general culture. A young student, whose playing has manifestly gained steadily in breadth of conception and poetic feeling, told me the other day that she attributed this largely to her reading in literature, art, and philosophy. Alas! there are few like her. The Conservatory students, with rare exceptions do not read, and consequently they do not think.

It should not be so. I am writing this in the hope that some of the alumni, who intend to send their children to Oberlin for musical study will give thought to their children's general education as well as to their musical education. The musical imagination, which is music power, does not live by music alone.

THE COMMENCEMENT PLAY

" The White Headed Boy," by Lennox Robinson, attracted and interested large audiences on Friday and Saturday evening. During the year the Dramatic Association, besides taking two long trips in the vacation periods, produced a number of one-act plays. A belated decision to have a single play for presentation at commencement forced a hurried preparation of this entertainment. Nevertheless the characterization was excellent and the action carried through without any slips. Those who have come to enjoy the delicate character portrayal and quiet humor of the newest Irish comedies were especially pleased with this year's commencement play.

ALUMNI NIGHT

Illumination Night was again the center of the festivities of commencement week. Although a decreased appropriation prevented some of the Illumination features which have been used before, the campus glowed with its usual beauty of Japanese lanterns. Nearly ten thousand people motored in from the surrounding country to enjoy the event and completely lined the streets on all four sides of the campus. The Alumni parade was the longest and best of Oberlin history, extending completely around the square.

Led by the 60-piece Girls' Band of Glenville High School, Cleveland, and the class of '13, which had secured it, the parade, with a continuous series of interesting floats, made its annual pilgrimage around the square. The banner for the best display was awarded the class of '98, which had a series of floats representing a marriage ceremony, followed by gifts which the class of '98 had given. Several of the other floats are described in the reports of class reunions. Among these notable for beauty were the displays of '93 and '08. Humor was added to the procession by the class of '22, which illustrated the need of a swimming pool by substituting a series of tanks in which mermen were enjoying themselves on a hot evening.

THE ALUMNI ASSOCIATION

The 84th Annual Meeting

The 84th annual meeting of the Alumni Association of Oberlin College was called to order at 9:30 Tuesday morning, June 19th. The floor of the First Church was crowded with alumni, principally from the reunion classes, whose members came in costume.

The presiding officer was Mr. Cleaveland R. Cross, '03, vice-president, who presided in the absence of President Mark L. Thomsen.

HONORARY MEMBERSHIP

Business was condensed in order to give ample time for discussion of the campaign (reported on page 7). An amendment to the constitution creating an honorary membership was passed, and later the nominating committee suggested the names of Mr. R. G. Peters, now ninety-one years old, the donor of Peters Hall, and the Rev. Jason Noble Pierce, author of "Ten Thousand Strong," our most popular song, as the first honorary members. They were unanimously elected. Another amendment granted associate membership to all present and former members of the faculty.

THE ALUMNAE AFFILIATION COMMITTEE

The alumni secretary reported that the Alumni Association had paid all dues and that now Oberlin is a member in full standing of the A. A. U. W.

Mrs. Helen W. Martin, chairman of the Alumnae Affiliation Committee, proposed the following alumnae as delegates and alternates for the National Conference of the American Association of University Women, to be held in Portland this July. The recommendation of the committee was unanimously carried.

DELEGATES TO THE THIRTY-EIGHTH ANNUAL CONVENTION OF THE A. A. U. W.
Mrs. Eva Emery Dye, Oregon City, Ore.
Mrs. Mary Plumb Millican, River Forest, Ill.
Mrs. Lucy Langdon Burwell, Seattle, Wash.
Mrs. Edith Francis Shahan, Parkdale, Ore.
Mrs. Marion Bridges Payne, Portland, Ore.
Mrs. Bess Hyde Whitcomb, Portland, Ore.
Mrs. Sarah Bailey Dunn, Portland, Ore.
Mrs. Helen Abbott Douglas, Portland, Ore.
Mrs. Anna Vetter Bassett, Edmonds, Wash.
Miss Jean McKercher, Portland, Ore.

ALTERNATES
Mrs. Nellie Moore Thompson, Milwaukee, Ore.
Mrs. Marion Bissell Webb, Oak Grove, Ore.
Mrs. Marguerite Hull Badger, Seattle, Wash.
Mrs. Josephine P. Reed, Aberdeen, Wash.
Mrs. Beth P. Lincoln, Pullman, Wash.
Miss M. M. Carson, Seattle, Wash.
Miss Alta Blood, Portland, Ore.

Mrs. Juanita Snyder Booth, Portland, Ore.
Mrs. Edith Robbins Strong, Seattle, Wash.
Mrs. Edith Rodman Bohler, Eugene, Wash.

ALUMNI MAGAZINE AND MEMBERSHIP

The alumni secretary reported that at least 3000 member-subscribers were essential to establish the alumni association on a sound financial basis. He reported that nearly all the women of the graduating class and more than half the men had already subscribed to the "Senior Budget," including subscription to the Association, to the Alumni Magazine, Living Endowment Union, and Shansi, but he called attention to the fact that even with these subscriptions there are less than 2500 subscribers to the magazine and 1900 members of the Alumni Association. It is hoped that ultimately every alumnus will subscribe to the magazine, and have some small share in the support of these other activities.

A WEEK-END COMMENCEMENT

The ballot taken at the Alumni Meeting showed a strong preference for a week-end Commencement, the vote standing 156 for the proposal and 31 for the present plan. The plan proposes, in brief, that Commencement be grouped primarily about four busy days: Friday, Senior Class day; Saturday, Alumni Day; Sunday, Baccalaureate; Monday, Commencement and Alumni Dinner. Objections from the alumni are due primarily it seems, to the fear that the time allowed is too brief for visiting. In practice, however, Commencement will really begin Thursday afternoon, and special reunions may well begin a day earlier and last a day later if further visiting is desired.

THE DIX OR GROUP REUNION PLAN

The vote on the Dix Reunion plan showed 145 in favor, with 24 against. Members of the classes of '03 and '04 who met together this year, apparently favor the scheme. Objections are raised by those classes whose fifth, fifteenth, twentieth, thirtieth, and fortieth reunions do not coincide with the scheme. There is, however, no slightest objection to such classes holding these decennial reunions if they wish, providing of course that they cooperate as fully as possible with the Dix plan.

Alumni Council Meeting

First Church,
Oberlin, O., June 19, 1923.

Owing to the illness of the president, Mr. Mark L. Thomsen, the meeting was called to order by the vice-president Mr. Cleaveland R. Cross.

Mr. W. S. Ament, secretary, gave a short report on the status of membership in the Association and the number of subscribers to the Alumni Magazine, these totalling about 1900 and 2500 subscribers. He asked the Council members for suggestions of ways to increase this number and also to incorporate into active membership in the Alumni Association all the chairmen (Division, State, District, Local, etc.) who are organized in such an effective way for conducting the endowment campaign

Mrs. A. W. Mastick of New York, suggested that subscribers to the Magazine be secured through the efforts of the campaign leaders.

Mr. W. S. Cochran of Cleveland, moved that it be considered essential to have every worker in the campaign a subscriber to the Magazine. Seconded by Mrs. Ruth Anderegg Frost of Pittsburgh. Carried.

Mr. Ament suggested that the very complete address lists of alumni and former students which have been secured through the campaign organization be published in place of the College Quinquennial. In addition he suggested that it would be a fine thing to continue the News Letter, sending it at least three times a year, possibly as follows: One issue after the opening of college in fall, one announcing Commencement plans and including an account of the February Council meeting; and another after Commencement.

Mr. F. C. Van Cleef of Hudson, moved that the idea of perpetuating the campaign address list as a catalogue be recommended to the college and that if the means could be found to continue the good work of the News Letter it should be done. Mr. B. M. Hogen of Salt Lake City seconded the motion. Carried.

Mr. Ament took occasion in the absence of Mr. Thomsen to speak of the interest and personal support which Mr. Thomsen has given the aims and efforts of the Alumni Association.

Mr. Ralph Cheney of Springfield, Mass., moved that such an appreciation be extended from the Council to Mr. Thomsen. Mr. Mark Ward of Toledo, seconded the motion. Carried.

On motion the meeting was adjourned.

Respectfully submitted,

MARIE W. WILSON.
Recording Secretary.

The following were present for the Council meeting June 19:

THE ALUMNI COUNCIL

Executive Committee:

Cleaveland R. Cross, '03
Mrs. Laura S. Price, '93
Marie W. Wilson. '14
Howard L. Rawdon. '04
Mrs. Helen W. Martin. '85
Mark O. Ward. '10
Mrs. Edna R. White. '08
William S. Ament, '10

Councilors at Large:

Grove H. Patterson. '05
Mrs. Mary P. Millikan. '93
Mrs. Agnes Warner Mastick '92
E. Allen Lightner, '03

Nominating Committee:

Heaton Pennington, Jr., '10
Mrs. Helen W. Martin, '85
'04 F. Van Cleef

Conservatory of Music-Councilors:

Miss Dorothy A. Badde, '22
James H. Hall. '15
Margaret Whipple Clark, '12

Class Councilors:

'74 David Nye. Elyria
'72 Adella Royce. Oberlin
'80 Mrs. W. W. Curtis. Oberlin
'83 Janet H. M. Swift. Oberlin
'91 Minnie Beard Siddall. East Cleveland
'92 Agnes W. Mastick. Pleasantville, N. Y.
'96 H. J. Hascell. Kansas City, Mo.
'97 V. O. Johnston. Oberlin
'98 Katharine Wright. Dayton
'02 Ellen P. Hatch. Oberlin
'03 Nelle Parsons Wright. Oberlin
'04 Rachel B. Rawdon. Oberlin
'05 Grove Patterson. Toledo
'06 William S. Cochran. Cleveland
'10 Heaton Pennington. Jr.. Cleveland
'13 Frances Jeffery Jones. Oberlin
'14 Marie W. Wilson. Cleveland
'21 P. H. Browning. Cleveland

Chapter Councilors:

Amy Reed Osborn. Cleveland
B. M. Hogen. Salt Lake City, Utah
Louis E. Hart. Chicago. Ill.
Mary Tenney Downing. Syracuse, N. Y.
C. E. Simpson. Detroit, Mich.
W. Harry Mack. Ann Arbor, Mich.
Ruth Anderegg Frost. Pittsburgh, Pa.
Carlos N. Bushnell. Buffalo, N. Y.
Ralph L. Cheney. Springfield, Mass.
Elizabeth Carpenter Thomas. Warren
R. W. Stratton. Norwalk
Mark O. Ward. Toledo

Professor P. D. Sherman gave the address at the Commencement exercises of the Ashtabula. Ohio, high school on June 14, when a class of 125 were graduated.

ATTENDANCE OF ALUMNI, REUNION CLASSES

The class of 1898 won the award of the Commencement Cup for the highest percentage of attendance of living alumni. Exactly 600 alumni were present from the fourteen classes holding special reunions. This is about 150 more than last year. The following table gives details:

	No. Living	No. Attending	Pct.
Class of 1898....	81	40	49.4
Class of 1922....	228	101	44.3
Class of 1913....	211	86	40.8
Class of 1893....	85	34	40.0
Class of 1903....	103	39	37.9
Class of 1918....	220	78	35.5
Class of 1883....	41	14	34.1
Class of 1888....	57	18	31.6
Class of 1908....	143	43	30.1
Class of 1921....	227	66	29.1
Class of 1878....	35	10	28.6
Class of 1873....	33	8	24.2
Class of 1904....	98	20	20.4
Class of 1920....	218	43	19.7
	1780	600	33.7

Professor C. B. Martin will spend the summer in lecturing on art and archæology under the auspices of the Bureau of University Travel. His itinerary includes England, Belgium, Holland, France, and Italy.

THE GOLDEN ANNIVERSARY OF '73

Eight members of the class of '73 gathered for their fiftieth reunion, using the Men's Building as their meeting place. Letters from Cyrus G. Baldwin and other classmates were read, and information about all classmates was brought up to date. Following the class picture (which turned out a failure because of double exposure), the heat of Tuesday afternoon was counteracted by an informal ice cream party. Following the class of '13 with their band, the class headed the Illumination Night parade comfortably seated in three automobiles. Mr. Willard Kimball, the second man to graduate from the Conservatory of Music, and founder of the Conservatory of Music at Grinnell and the University School of Music at Lincoln, Nebr., represented the class at the Alumni Dinner.

Those present were Hale G. Parker, Chicago; Willard Kimball, Lincoln, Nebr.; A. H. Kennedy, Rockport, Ind.; Mrs. Herbert H. Wright, Elyria, O.; Mrs. Arthur H. Perry, Berea, O.; M. I. Todd, Wakeman, O.; Alexander Hadden, Cleveland, O.; Sarah Edwards Jones, Canfield, O.

Other alumni present who studied in Oberlin College before 1873 were Adella N. Royce, '72, Oberlin; Mrs. Elizabeth Keep Clark, '69, Evanston, Ill.; Wlastimil Swaty, '69-'71, Cleveland; Mrs. Marion Wood Merrill, '70, Oberlin; R. T. Cross, '67, Twinsburg, O.; T. G. Newton, '71, Cleveland; Mrs. Rachel Chambers Hanby, '66, Bucyrus, O.; Celia Burr, '70, Oberlin; Lucien C. Warner, '65, New York.

THE CLASS GIFT

The gift of the Senior class this year was an additional $300.00 towards the so-called "rose window" for the chapel. When it was found that the original design for a rose window would be altogether beyond the reach of a series of class gifts, Architect Cass Gilbert was asked to make a new design. This did not reach Oberlin College in time for the class of '22 to take action upon it and consequently the gift last year took the form of a moving picture. By the gift of one more class the cost of the new design will be covered and doubtless the stained glass window will be in place within the next two or three years.

JUBILEE CLASS—1883

From California, Massachusetts, Florida, and the states between the members of '83 gathered for their fortieth reunion. Mrs. Clarence F. Swift (Nettie McKelvey) and W. V. Metcalf ("Billy") had served efficiently in their labor of love to get the class together. Fairchild House had been secured for headquarters, and decorated with class colors and numeral. Rooms and board had been arranged for also, and when sixteen, then twenty, then twenty-two of the class reported from all departments, the reunion was sure to be a success.

There was a delightful informal gathering on Mrs. Swifth's lawn Sunday afternoon, when she served as hostess. The announced reunion Tuesday afternoon was held back of Fairchild House, Edwin Slater of Minneapolis, well known attorney and long-time friend of the college, being toastmaster. Before taking seats for the banquet a memorial service was held for those who have passed away since graduation, seventeen in all. Special mention was made of a number whose lives had been abundantly fruitful in their lines of service, and a prayer of remembrance accompanied the words of loving regard.

In connection with the banquet an hour of reminiscences was enjoyed, a number of letters also being read from those who could not attend.

Not only had headquarters been decorated outside, but in the parlor had been collected a large number of photographs of the class members during college days and after, and also of their children and grandchildren.

Eighty-three's part in the parade was one worthy of the Jubilee class. A large banner was carried by Mrs. Swift and James Fairchild in the lead. Handsome national flags followed, and large mottos—"Service for Country," "Service for College," "Service for Home," "Service for God," with a transparancy bearing the class numeral and "Jubilee Class," making the display effective.

The various Commencement events were attended by the class in a body. Mrs. Swift was elected president, or councilor of the class, and W. V. Metcalf, secretary and treasurer. Now '83 will anticipate and plan for its own golden jubilee in 1933, the 100th of the college.

C. D. W. BROWER.

'93 HAS NOTABLE REUNION

Thirty-four of the living members of the class of '93 returned to the thirtieth reunion of their class; and this number, augmented by three ex-members, the husbands and wives, the twenty-two children and three class relatives, made a total of seventy-six who sat down to the class supper on Tuesday evening. The first formal appearance was made at the Faculty reception Monday afternoon when they captured the situation at once with their class yell and the song which ended with the line, "'93· Look at us and see the best." With Dr. C. E. Briggs as honorary marshal; E. Dana Durand among the trustees; Mary Plumb Millikan, and Ruth Savage, a daughter of the class, speakers at the alumni meeting Tuesday morning; Louis E. Hart, the representative at the alumni dinner; and above all, with Henry Cowles, a recipient of the degree of Sc.D., for his distinguished work in the field of plant ecology, the class felt less keenly their failure to win more than honorable mention in the alumni parade and their falling short of the requisite number to give them the cup.

White costumes and Japanese umbrellas made them conspicuous wherever they went, and won them applause in the parade as they followed the float. A globe six feet in diameter, covered with white peonies and encircled with a legend in the class colors, "Oberlin founded in 1833, famed by 1893," was mounted on a motor lorry covered with tamarack branches and guarded by four of the daughters of '93· This as well as the umbrellas were the result of Mary Plumb Millikan's and Louis E. Hart's planning, and to them was due a large part of the pleasure of the week. To many the happiest hours were those spent on the lawn and porch of headquarters through the day, and early evening; and later, till midnight, in groups up and down stairs. Mrs. Gulde and Mrs. Paddock and her daughter, as hostesses, made a free and kindly atmosphere, in which old acquaintance was renewed and strengthened, and new ties formed with the children of the class.

ETTA M. WRIGHT.

Professor J. F. Mack delivered Commencement addresses at Niles and at Valley City, Ohio, early in June. He also gave the Decoration Day address at Amherst, Ohio.

"The Ship of Golden Dreams"

PLUCKY '88

The success of the 35th reunion of '88 was assured before we arrived by the careful planning of the local committee. Headquarters had been secured at 151 North Professor Street, the home of Lois Campbell Klinefelter, '85, whose courtesy and tireless efforts for our comfort were large factors in the pleasure of our reunion. Here we hung the historic white and gold flags of '88.

Mary Harbach Lynch arrived June 12, and we kept coming until Mrs. Arthur Griffith joined us Commencement day, representing Art, who could not come. We did not win the cup, for we had only 31% of our 57 living graduates present. But Walter Hayden, who was with us several years, came, and wives, husbands and children brought our numbers to 34. Several members of classes not renning joined us. We had no grandchildren present, but we are the proud possessors of a large number of most remarkable ones!

After Baccalaureate we had a buffet supper at Lillie Thompson Terborgh's. Our reunion banquet, with speeches and letters and a reverent memorial for our dead, was held Tuesday evening at Mrs. Klinefelter's.

We had modest plans for appearing in the alumni parade, our aged selves enthroned comfortably in a hay wagon. But we reckoned without that youthful and agile grandmother, Agnes Fairchild Kirshner, who arrived Monday full of brilliant ideas. With some assistance she turned our hay wagon into what *every one*—except the judges—declared was the best float in the parade! A stately white ship—"Our Ship of Golden Dreams," with wide red sail. Enthroned were three majestic figures of Faith, Hope, Love, and by the center mast were heaped great golden bags, labelled in millions. John Commons, Charlie Chamberlain and Bob Paton walked beside it, holding red flags, and the rest of us, in white and gold, followed, holding baskets from which we threw "golden" coins.

Nettie Munson called "Ship Ahoy! Ship Ahoy!" and we answered, "This is the Ship of Golden Dreams!" "Who's the Lookout?" "Faith at the prow." "Who's the Captain?" "Hope on the bridge." "Who's the Pilot?" "Love at the helm." "What's the cargo?" "Four and a half millions for Oberlin!" Then the song—

"We're coming, Mother Oberlin, full sixteen thousand strong,
To show our fond devotion by our loving
gifts and song!
With Faith and Hope and Love as guides
we're sailing right along—
Our Ship of Golden Dreams! "

When you see the picture of that float (50
cents from Lillie Thompson Terborgh) you
will agree that we should have had *both*
prizes!

The reunion brought us many delights, one
of the greatest the arrival of Amy Bridgman
Cowles from seven years in Africa. We had
our honors, too—Lillie's daughter, Ruth, graduated and made Phi Beta Kappa. That has
become a habit with Lill's children! There
were already two Phi Beta's among them.
And proudly we watched Charlie Chamberlain
made a Doctor of Science, while President
King said most complimentary things about
him.

Sadness came, too, in the death on Tuesday
of Alice Williams' mother.

To all of us the long quiet hours of talk
were best—tales of old days, stories of our
successes and our failures, of our work, our
pleasures, and our hope in our children. These
draw us close in friendship, and we longed to
have all the rest with us.

A full account of the reunion, with letters
and news of every one, will later be sent to
all members of the class.

NELL DOWNING COMMONS.

'93 CHALLENGES ALL CLASSES

Replying to the not very modest remarks
of Frank P. Whitney, who represented '98 at
the alumni dinner, telling the world about the
achievements of '98, Louis E. Hart, '93, in
turn challenged '98 and every other class to
equal the percent of the members of '93 who
will pledge to the Campaign. The contest is
on, and the race to see which class has the
largest proportion of loyal members (for the
amounts given are not considered) will bear
close watching. What is your class going
to do?

Miss Mabel C. Eldred will spend the summer at the University of Wisconsin.

THE PRIZE CLASS, '98

Forty members of the class of '98 were present to celebrate their 25th reunion. Most of
these stayed at May Cottage on Elm Street,
which had been engaged for class headquarters.
A few visited relatives or friends in town.

A feature of the reunion was the large number of wives, husbands and children present.
These added greatly to the interest of the
gathering. At the class dinner on Tuesday,
when an effort was made to get together, eighty
were present.

For the second time '98 won the banner
given the class making the best showing in
the Alumni Parade. The attendance of forty
out of eighty-one living members, making a
percentage of 49.4, also won the Alumni Cup
for 1923.

Mark Thomsen, president of the Alumni Association, who was prevented from coming
sooner on account of sudden illness, arrived
Wednesday morning in time to join the class
before the members began to scatter. G. Harrison Durand, vice-president of Yankton College, stopped over night and for breakfast on
his way to Montreal, whence he sailed for Europe a few days later.

It was a matter of great regret to all that
John Siddall, on whom the college conferred
the degree of Master of Arts, was unable to
be present on account of illness. The degree
was given *in absentia.*

As a class distinction the women and girls
wore tunics of the class colors, crimson and
grey; the men and boys wore neckties of the
same colors. All wore white duck hats with
bands of the colors.

The officers of the class for the next five
years are Katharine Wright, president; Lucien T. Warner, secretary and treasurer.

ALUMNAE SONG CONTEST

Although twenty-five or thirty songs were
submitted for the Alumnae Song Contest, none
seemed to be of sufficient merit to warrant its
adoption as the special song for the women of
Oberlin College. Consequently the date for the
closing of the contest has been postponed until April 1 next. The prizes remain the same,
and songs already submitted may be revised
for the final contest. Songs should be sent
care of the Alumni Office, Oberlin, Ohio.

'03 AND '04

The class of 1903, which held a joint reunion with the class of 1904, had its quinquennial business meeting on Tuesday at the Vatican. '03 headquarters. It elected as its officers Mr. Allan Lightner as secretary and executive officer and Mrs. Elizabeth Jackson Stewart as councilor of the Alumni Association.

Mr. Lightner is known and appreciated not only by the members of his own class, but a great many of the alumni knew "Happy," and many remember his work as a baseball player and his part among the tenors of the Glee Club.

Miss Mary Cochran, the retiring officer, has been the prime mover in most of '03's affairs. In fact she has been the central figure holding the cards that lead out to widely separated members and drawing them back to their Alma Mater.

Mrs. Stewart has been one of the most enthusiastic and untiring helpers in work for this twentieth reunion and Oberlin and her interests are very dear to her. The class are glad to entrust their part in the association to her.

'03 thoroughly enjoyed this first joint reunion and are enthusiastically for the Dix plan.

The Sunday evening gathering at the home of Mr and Mrs. Wirkler was one of the most enjoyable occasions of the week. This is one more thing that Mr. Wirkler has added to the best of things done by Jack for '03 and the alumni in general.

At the banquet Tuesday there were present 127. Of this number 34 were members of '03. 26 of '04. The rest included the families and a few of '01 and '02.

AFTERNOON PUNCH

The so-called Alumni-Faculty Tea at 4:00 o'clock on Monday this year took the form of a general alumni reunion lubricated by punch. The faculty committee on commencement has voted to transfer this tea to the Art Building and to make of it a genuine President's and Faculty Reception to the Alumni. It should be one of the pleasantest features of the commencement next year.

'08 HAS BEAUTIFUL FLOAT

1908 was back at Allencroft 45 strong, with 10 "in-laws" and 30 children to swell the throng. On the living room table was a kodak-book showing 50 classmates, their haunts, their families and what not. There too were various musical and literary productions of different members of the class and a special kodak-book for those who are no longer living. For distinction the class wore replicas of the crimson and black banner slung from shoulder to shoulder, back and front, the point falling below the waist. To Mary Hobbs of the Cleveland group belongs the entire credit for these very effective banners, the 160 of them being a permanent contribution to our reunion paraphernalia.

The dinner, "Tom" Sawyer presiding, with Professor and Mrs. Root, Miss Fitch and Mrs. Robson as honor guests, went off merrily. There were excerpts from letters and other messages from absentees, including telegrams from Buck Ferris, George Everson, and Floy Stone, and nonsense jingles about those present. Frank Dudley read from his own verses, and there were songs, the gem of the occasion being Winifred Jensen Stedman's Cow-Song.

Claude Stedman's float was an artistic triumph. At one end, in the person of Stella Eikenberry Risinger was a color reproduction of Kenyon Cox's lunette recently adopted as Oberlin Alma Mater. Children with uplifted gifts expressed the idea now uppermost in the Oberlin mind. The float was surrounded by more children. Preceding and following the brilliantly lighted float were massed the somberly bannered classmates, bearing aloft parchment shaded torches. Along the side lines, in medieval fashion cavorted the traditional '08 cow with glaring eye and tail lights. It was led by Bud Waters—Birdie and Hugh Smith were inside.

The elections resulted as follows: Class secretary (the executive officer), Mary Ellis Purcell Lester; class councilor, Art Bradley; treasurer, Grover Hull.

"PIE NIGHT" WINS PRIZE

The prize of $100 offered for the best original operetta on an Oberlin theme was awarded to a revised form of "Pie Night." The catchy words of this operetta were written by F. Earl Ward, '22, and the tuneful music by Lewis H. Horton, Conservatory.

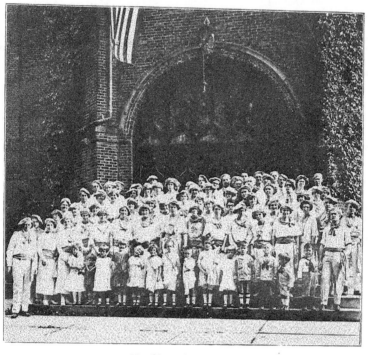

The Class of '13 in Blue and White

COMMENCEMENT ACTIVITIES OF THE CLASS OF 1913

From the time of the arrival of the first contingent at class headquarters at Dascomb Cottage, to the closing song at the Reunion Glee Club concert the members of 1913 participated in the best planned and most enjoyable reunion yet held. Eighty-six of the 211 living members of the class answered the call for the tenth reunion,—taking third place, with a percentage of 40%, in the Attendance Cup award. More than 125 classmates, wives, husbands and children ate together in the old Second Church Building at the reunion supper.

To 1913 was given the honor of leading the parade on Illumination Night,—an honor given chiefly because 1913 possessed a band. Through the efforts of Mrs. Matie Merrill Parker and E. C. Theller (a member of the class by marriage) the Girls' Band of the Glenville High School of Cleveland was present with sixty instruments. The band, under the capable direction of Mr. Griffith Jones, entertained the

class during the reunion supper, rendered an attractive musical program in connection with the President's Reception, led the parade, and featured in the musical exercises on the steps at Finney Chapel.

The class made a most pleasing appearance with their distinctions of blue caps and sashes with white numerals, and blue scarfs. The float displayed the seal of the College, surrounded by six large candles, grouped about which were couples depicting six epochs of Oberlin's life. Two children represented the epoch of the future in 1933.

Of unusual merit was the speech made at the Alumni Dinner by the class representative, Professor Jerome Davis of Dartmouth College. In a vivid and compelling manner Mr. Davis reminded his hearers of Oberlin's great pioneering record, in the championing of unpopular causes, and then challenged the Oberlin of the present to dare to pioneer in the realm of social justice and international good will.

Officers for the next five years were elected

as follows: President, Earle W. Derr; vice-president, Celia Scoby Clarke; secretary, Leroy Griffith; treasurer, Carlos N. Bushnell; councilor, Claude Clarke.

1918 REUNION AND THE HUDSON SCHOLARSHIP

"18's Back" was the doubly significant and extremely accurate orange and black message which rode around the village of Oberlin attached to the rear of all of the "Eighteen's" Fords and Packards. From the Atlantic, the Pacific, and the Gulf coasts they assembled, until 1918 had 78 members to answer roll call. With them came, of course, wives or husbands, or rumors of such, and adorable babies. Some of the youngsters did not choose to appear in person, but at least they sent their pictures so there was quite a family gathering.

Orange silk handkerchiefs with black picot edge, worn in leather wrist straps by the girls and in upper vest pockets by the men, formed the rather attractive insignia which served to separate the sheep from the goats on all but special occasions, when any possible doubt was removed by the addition of orange and black crêpe paper hats.

Tuesday was the great day. In the afternoon the class, with varying emotions, saw themselves as they used to be, and after the 500 feet of precious film was back in its box they agreed that even Earl Parks could still be recognized. Tuesday evening came the special banquet served on the porch at Grey Gables, and that night 1918 ventured forth again into the world of competition with its float, courageous men forming the van and rear guard and generous women the central idea. The demonstration won great applause but not the banner so that the real excitement of the evening was furnished by the 1918 ladies who fell backwards off the top row of the bleachers and were put together again by the rather new 1918 doctors.

The presentation of the Henry Burt Hudson Memorial Scholarship Fund, with its formal acceptance by President King in the name of Oberlin College at the alumni banquet Wednesday noon, was the crowning event which concluded the fifth reunion.

In memory of "Red" Hudson, athlete, scholar, and well loved classmate, who was burned to death in the flames of his falling aeroplane in France in 1918, the class gave to Oberlin College $2500. From this fund a scholarship, now

amounting to $125 and to be increased to $250 during the next five years, will be awarded each year to the Junior man who is recommended by the College Committee on Scholarships and is elected by vote of the Men's Senate.

Henry B. Hudson 18

It was a glorious reunion, and the class wants to thank not only those of its members who were particularly responsible in helping to make it so, but also its friends, among whom Billy Ament, Azariah Root and George M. Jones deserve most special mention.

FRANCES BROWN

ALUMNI DINNER

The Alumni Dinner proved unusually popular this year, forcing the college to provide for an overflow of 140 people at Talcott. In spite of the extreme heat, 1,200 alumni, including seniors and their parents, listened to a long series of speeches, notable among which were Jerome Davis's appeal for a revival of the old crusading spirit to place Oberlin in the van of those seeking social and international justice and good will. Louis E. Hart, '93, challenged all of the classes of the college to equal the percentage of '93 in support of the coming campaign. Mr. Paul D. Cravath, '82, spoke enthusiastically of the new Oberlin which has emerged under the leadership of President King. Dr. Paul Elmer More, the Commencement speaker, made a significant plea for scholarship which, however, was largely lost in the heat and confusion of the late afternoon.

OUR FIRST REUNION

One hundred and two strong, of the class of '22, responded to the call of Commencement of their Alma Mater. School teachers, junior clerks, salesmen, ice boys, and many future bank presidents came to forget the worries and care of the year and be jolly and carefree Freshman-Alumni. We knew that we were to be seen and not heard—but why worry about that?

Johnson House was assigned as headquarters, and thirty girls took possesion. The men were told that they would have to look elsewhere, so we parked on the campus, the chairs at the M. B., or on the edge of the bed of a lucky friend. Nevertheless, we did not have as much trouble as many of the alumni; we could easily recognize our friends of the previous year—no bald heads, bungalow front porches, or youngsters have put in their appearnce as yet.

Monday night we tripped the light fantastic with the rest of the alumni. Tuesday morning the girls breakfasted together at the Johnson House, and at night seventy banqueted at Hobbs'. Fans and handkerchiefs came in handy. Our professional railroaders assisted in a class meeting and everything went off in grand style. Dues of one dollar each were assessed to help finance the Class Letter, which will be published January 1, 1924. All members are to write a letter and send it to Harry M. Will, 3200 Franklin Avenue, Cleveland, O., Class Secretary, on or before December, 1923. Theodore Soller and the writer were reëlected as Alumni Representative and Class Secretary.

We entered two floats on Illumination Night. One as "Talcott Tree" and the other a miniature swimming pool. The crowd seemed to misunderstand our efforts to cool the atmosphere for in nearly all cases they backed away from the curb.

At the alumni meeting and alumni dinner we learned of the campaign for $4,500,000 and that we were each to get or give only $285.00. Where will get it? No one knows—but when the time comes we will have it. Four years at Oberlin and you find that you are Oberlin's forever! What is $285.00? Oh, you can just bet, Alumni, that we are proud that we decided to attend Oberlin, and that Oberlin decided to graduate us. We may seem insignificant—but here's a tip—"WATCH US GROW!"

HARRY WILL.

PHI KAPPA PI

The second love feast of the revived Phi Kappa Pi proved without a doubt that the society is back on the campus to stay. After dinner speeches were given by Mr. Archer H. Shaw, '97, of the Cleveland *Plain Dealer*, Frank C. Van Cleef, '04, of the Goodrich Rubber Co., Akron, J. Harold Wilson, '22, who has finished his first year as teacher at Syracuse University, and Wilbur O. Lewis, '23, who reviewed the work of the past year.

In behalf of an unnamed donor the Alumni Secretary presented a silver loving cup as a perpetual trophy to be held by the winner of an annual public speaking contest. The winner of the contest this year was Mr. Norman Shaw, '26, and in his absence the cup was presented to Mr. Archer H. Shaw, his father.

Mr. Wayne B. Wheeler of '94 presided over a parliamentary drill, which became too complex for even his skillful management. Between the intervals of drill and fun Mr. E. Dana Durand, '93, of Washington, D. C., spoke briefly on the value of complete freedom of speech in public debate. Merritt Starr, '75, commented on the action of the trustees in regard to the campaign and gave a spirited appeal for each Oberlin alumnus to support the great campaign; Mr. Wayne B. Wheeler described the great series of debates concerning the prohibition movement which he has been conducting, the greatest one of which was broadcasted to 300,000 people by radio. Mr. Wheeler emphasized the necessity of supporting the majority and the laws passed by the majority, until through public argument a minority could itself become a majority. He reported that in response to the broadcasted debate more than two-thirds of the letters written favor the strict enforcement of the dry amendment; and finally Mr. Bruce R. Baxter, '15, who has just returned from a trip to the Near East, brought a message of cheer and confidence in the ultimate goodness of human character in spite of the confusion in the world today.

The meeting was an unqualified success and the future of public speaking and of the societies in Oberlin is assured. In all probability one of the other two literary societies will be revived next year.

'84, A.M. '95—Rev. George B. Waldron has accepted a pastorate in Mounds, Ill.

THE OLD TIMERS
Standing—McGill, '19; Maize, Cons.; Wiley, Ex-'08; Todd, '06; Waters, '08;
Clancy, '97: Smith, '08; Smiley, '20·
Seated—Williams, 'ex-'22; Nichols, '11; Smythe, Ex-'02; Lightner, '03; Lappin, '15;
Hoopes, '05; Vradenburg, '10; Wilcox, Ex-'97; Andrews, '21·

VARSITY 9—ALUMNI 6

With a motley collection of alumni stars, dating well back in the nineties, the Alumni-Varsity baseball game turned out to be a pageant of twenty-five years of baseball.

Ross Wiley, ex-'08, one of the best pitchers Oberlin ever produced, turned out for the first time in seventeen years, and pitched fine ball for the first four innings. Wiley has had many experiences since leaving Oberlin, including trips to South America and the Far West. He is now settled down as a farmer down in the state. In spite of his heady pitching Varsity scored five runs during the first four innings, while Weber held the oldsters scoreless.

Wiley was replaced by "Whit" Andrews, the left-handed star of two years ago, and George Vradenburg replaced "Lou" Todd behind the bat. Although the new battery was even more effective than the first, Varsity squeezed across four more runs, and not until the ninth inning did the alumni really get started on their offensive play. With a sudden batting rally the alumni scored five runs, and had three men on bases, with "Herb" Nichols at bat. At this crucial moment Coach Keller removed Houck, who had begun to weaken, and brought in again from center field, Weber, one of the best pitchers in Ohio. With the record standing 3

and 2 Weber forced Nichols to imitate the famous Casey, and the game was over. The surprising fact about the game was the remarkable throwing of the alumni, who cut off three runs at the plate and several others on bases. With a slower pitcher in the box the alumni would have given the Varsity a closer run for the game.

The oldest players on the field were Judge Wilcox, '97· of the Probate Court of Elyria, O., at second, and "Bib" Clancy, '97· at short. "Bud" Waters proved to be the Nick Altrock of the solemn occasion, while George Vradenburg was there with "the old fight."

Professor W. L. Carr, an alumnus of Drake University, was invited to become one of the foundation members of the new chapter of Phi Beta Kappa, which was installed there April 19, 1923. He gave the Phi Beta Kappa address at the dinner which followed the initiation of undergraduate candidates and other alumni on May 30. His subject was "What is an Education?" Professor Carr has recently been elected secretary of the Classical Association of the Middle West and South to succeed Dean Rollin H. Tener, of Denison University, who has been called to New York University.

"O" CLUB BANQUET

The Varsity "O" Club banquet was for the second time held in the Men's Building, this year in the Commons dining room. Sixty-one "O" men sat down to a substantial dinner provided by Herr Bischoff. On account of the extreme heat the baseball games on the lawn in front of the building, which were to have preceded the dinner, were omitted, but nevertheless the athletes seemed able to do justice to the meal. Representatives from the reunion classes were called upon for reminiscences. Lou Hart of the famous '93 football team was the first speaker. Others who followed were E. A. Lightner, '03, baseball; Bud Waters, '08, three sport men; Harry Colmery, '13, baseball; Ed Cheney, '18, football. Mr. Cheney paid a remarkable tribute to Red Hudson and announced that the class of '18 had set out to raise a scholarship fund of $5000, which was to be known as the "Red Hudson Scholarship." Without exception the old grad speakers were enthusiastic over Oberlin's athletics and almost all urged upon the group the necessity of interesting redblooded young men to come to Oberlin.

Reese Rickards, football captain, Art Winters, basketball captain, Bruce Gorsuch, track captain, and Bob Jamieson baseball captain, were called upon to say a word about the sports of the present year, and Coaches Stallings and McPhee responded briefly to a few questions concerning the present year and prospects for next year. Director Savage, who was in charge of the program, briefly reviewed the year in both intercollegiate and intramural sport, and invited questions or suggestions concerning the athletic interests of Oberlin.

MASS MEETINGS

The experiment of mass meetings for alumnae and alumni was justified this year in spite of the lateness of the hour by the interesting and valuable programs.

The women sang songs submitted by representatives of the eight different campaign districts in the United States and compared slogans which are to be used in the fall. The best of the slogans was that of the New England division, "Leave no stone unturned save Plymouth Rock." Since no song for the Alumnae Song Contest secured the approval of the judges the contest has been extended until next April, the prizes remaining the same.

At the men's mass meeting, besides the rousing singing of several college songs, Harold Wood, president of the graduating class, presented the advance in the life of the man during his years in college. He spoke very highly of the unifying effect upon the Freshman class of boarding together at the Commons and also favored the smaller houses for groups of upper class men. Speaking on the subject, "The Life of the Men from the Point of View of the Alumni," Mr. Louis E. Hart, '93, of Chicago, urged a greater degree of coöperation among the alumni, the establishment of more alumni clubs, and more entertainment of undergraduates by the alumni.

The whole meeting was a step in advance towards a completer men's life at Oberlin College.

THE GRAY MEMORIAL SCHOLARSHIP

The Alumni-Varsity basketball game on February 21 made it possible for the Gray Memorial Fund to carry two scholars during the next college year. Mr. James Parsons of Lakewood, the first Gray Memorial Scholar, will be continued, and Mr. Charles Hunsche of Akron, has received an appointment for the class of '27. Mr. Hunsche stands third in scholarship among the men of the senior class at Akron Central High School, and was highly recommended for the many qualifications desired for the Gray Scholar. He has been active in the High Y work and he has a good record in track and baseball.

SIGMA GAMMA LOVE FEAST

The annual Love Feast of Sigma Gamma was held at the James Brand House on Monday evening, June 18, with fifty members present. The following "Rainbow" program was given, with Lena Forster, '23, as toastmistress: The Primary Colors, Mrs. H. W. Niederhauser, '13; The Color of the Dawn (harp music), Martha Eglin; The Message of the Rainbow, Marie Wilson, '14; The Bow of Promise, Greta Bellows, '24; The Pot of Gold, Dr. Florence M. Fitch.

New officers were elected as follows: President, Mary Zay Blackford, '13; vice-president, Frances Jeffrey Jones, '13; secretary-treasurer, Lena Forster, '23. The treasurer reports a balance of $26.24 in the bank.

Athletics

Norman Shaw '26

The four weeks' record shows seven victories, one defeat, first in a triangle, and second in a state, meet.

BASEBALL

Three games and three victories is the Oberlin record for the month. One game was cancelled.

OBERLIN 6—HIRAM 5

Hiram College arrived with a pitcher who was supposed to be nearly invincible, but seven hits and six runs were enough to give the victory to Oberlin. Hiram started in the first inning with one run off Gurney, and then took four more in the second. But he tightened, and Oberlin came back strong in the fourth with five runs. The extra run was scored in the seventh.

OBERLIN 6—DENISON 3

With the biggest margin of victory of any game of the season up till that time, Oberlin walloped the Granville outfit 6 to 3. Oberlin scored three in the first, were tied in the third, but finished another three in the fourth. Gurney and Weber pitched, the latter striking out nine and passing none in six innings.

OBERLIN 10—HIRAM 2

The final intercollegiate game of the season was too much of a walk away to be interesting. Oberlin hit for ten hits and seven runs in the first inning, and later added three. Weber was the star of the game, with sixteen strikeouts, three hits and two runs. Captain Jamieson was rather seriously injured when a pitched ball hit him in the eye, and Reither was spiked in the same game.

TRACK

The important event of the month was the Big Six held at Columbus. Wesleyan won this event, scoring 49½ points. Oberlin was a close second with 40½ points, Miami third with 37½, and Case fourth with 25½. Wood of Oberlin was the star, scoring two firsts in the discus and the high jump. Channon won second in the javelin, Richardson second in the 440, and Williams second in the mile. Captain Gorsuch failed to place better than third and fourth in the 100 and 220. Breaks went against Oberlin, and bad luck in lottery for starting places was

partly responsible for the score, although McPhee ran up against real competition with the Wesleyan aggregation. Oberlin came second in the relay, arriving four feet behind the Wesleyan man.

OBERLIN 80—DENISON 51

Winning twelve firsts and the mile relay, Oberlin secured ample revenge for the Denison track victory of last year. Oberlin won practically all the track events, many of them in close races. Hopkins captured both hurdles, breaking one Denison record.

OBERLIN 90½—MT. UNION 39—RESERVE 32½

This triangular meet held on Dill Field proved to be one of the best events of the season although Oberlin nearly doubled on the combined points of her two opponents. Oberlin took ten firsts, and in many of them records came near falling. Smith in the broad jump lacked only an inch of the 22-foot record, and in the 100 and 220 Gorsuch was each time one-fifth second behind.

TENNIS

Three victories, a tie and one defeat is the record of Coach Bill Parkhill's raqueters for the month. In the first match Oberlin took on the University of Pittsburgh for a return event, and tied them 3-3. Landis and McKibben won singles and Landis-Knight doubles. The following week Oberlin had no difficulty in whitewashing Heidelberg winning every event for a 6-0 score. Reserve was next on the list, losing 4-2 after winning the first two matches. On Decoration Day Michigan Aggies lost out by a 3-1 score. Denison, however, proved a jinx, and won every event except Knight's singles. In the state meet at Columbus Oberlin was runner up in the doubles, but failed to get far in singles.

On May 22 Professor Holmes addressed about 150 high school seniors of Medina county at an "On to College" banquet. On June 11 Professor Holmes lectured at the University of Chicago on "Some Applications of Colloid Chemistry." From June 12 to June 15 he attended a Colloid Symposium at the University of Wisconsin, where he read a paper on "The Formation of Gels."

News of the Alumni

'61—Mrs. Henry E. Brown (Lucy Eveline Sparhawk) died at Demorest, Ga., June 19. The funeral was held June 23 in Oberlin, where Mrs. Brown had made her home until about a year ago. She was born in Norton, Ohio, June 30, 1839, and married Henry E. Brown, a college classmate, April 21, 1863. Mr. Brown died in May, 1922.

'63—Everel Spencer Smith died at his home in Westville, Ind., May 30, at the age of 84. He was the last living man of his class.

'64—James C. Cannon of Honolulu, Hawaii, died May 20, 1923.

'68—Professor C. B. Bradley of Berkeley, Calif., has been invited to London to read a paper before the Royal Asiatic Society on the occasion of its hundredth anniversary. His subject is to be some phase of the life-long Siamese studies. Professor Bradley has the honor of being the highest authority on the Siamese language and literature in the world. He sailed for England the last of June.

Acad. '73-'74—Willis E. Biggs, for many years a resident of Clarinda, Iowa, died at his home, after a lingering illness, on May 23.

'83—Rev. C. De W. Brower of Tampa, has been elected by the Florida Conference of Congregational Churches as Moderator for the ensuing year.

'86, T. '90, A.M. '90, D.D. '11—President Laurence L. Doggett of Springfield Y. M. C. A. College, Mass., on May 18 announced the gift of $500,000 to the college from the Laura Spellman Rockefeller Memorial Foundation in New York. The college closes an expansion fund campaign for $2,000,000 July 1.

T. '88—Rev. E. P. Harding has resigned his pastorate at Marblehead, Ohio.

'89-'94—Rev. Edwin Booth, Jr., of Charles City, Iowa, has accepted a call to the Community Church, Manitou, Colo.

'90, A.M. '96, D.D. '15—Dr. Warren H. Wilson, Director of Church and Country Life of the Board of Home Missions of the Presbyterian Church and professor of Rural Economics at Columbia University, taught two courses at the Summer School for Pastors at Ohio State University June 18 to July 5.

'91—Mrs. Judith Carter Horton of Guthrie, Okla., has been appointed by Governor Walton a member of the governing board of the Orphans School at Taft. Mrs. Horton is one of the most prominent colored club women of the state. For several years she was the president of the Oklahoma Federation of Negro Women's Clubs, and for many years has been the librarian in Excelsior Library in Guthrie. Her appointment to this new position is expected to mean a thorough investigation into the management of the Orphans School.

'94—Edgar P. Stocker, son of Charles J. Stocker of Cleveland, and a senior at Dartmouth this year, is one of the winners of the George E. Chamberlain fellowship, which entitles him to study at any university he may choose for the next two years. Mr. Stocker expects to study political science and history at Columbia.

'96—Gail T. Abbott was notified that his son, Richard, had been appointed a cadet at West Point Military Academy and to report there July 2 to begin his training. His oldest daughter just completed her third year in the Conservatory. Another daughter, Helen, is a sophomore at Ohio State University, taking a course in Domestic Science.

'96—George F. White has been elected president of the Congregational Club of Cleveland and vicinity for next year. The Club has a record of forty-eight years and there are some two hundred members.

C. '97—Mary Houghton Brown, who is teaching piano in New York, has recently appeared with success in several concerts there. On May 10 she played in the recital given by members of the Washington Heights Musical Club at Æolian Hall. By request the program is to be repeated at the Wanamaker auditorium in October. Miss Brown is also on the club program to be given at Æolian Hall in March of next season.

'98—Franklin H. Warner, with Mrs. Warner and Lucien H. Warner, '22, were in Shansi for a week, May 14-21, visiting the work of their classmate, W. A. Hemingway, M.D., and also the Oberlin work in Shansi. Mrs. Warner is the president of the Woman's Board of Missions of the Congregational Church.

'98-'05—Marion Elizabeth Comings, formerly of the Cleveland Museum of Art, is now with the Art Institute of Chicago.

T. '00—Rev. Elisha A. King is pastor of the Miami Beach, Fla., church. The church was founded two years ago with a membership of

28. There are now 55 members, who have recently succeeded in raising a budget of $7,500. Mr. King is this summer conducting a lecture-study class on "Evolution and Christian Faith," which has aroused a great deal of interest and is especially significant in view of the agitation on the subject in the South.

'01—Rev. Seeley K. Tompkins has accepted a call to the Central Congregational Church, Boston, Mass. He has been pastor of the Campello Church, Brockton. He succeeds Dr. W. L. Sperry, who was last year made dean of the School of Theology of Harvard University.

'01—Jessie A. Hyde died in Albuquerque, N. Mex., November 4, 1922, of acute asthma. Miss Hyde's home was in Warren, Ohio, where her father is an attorney. After her graduation from Oberlin she taught school in Youngstown, Ohio. Later she took a course in settlement work at Harvard University and did work in this field in New York City. For some time before her death she had lived in the west in an endeavor to benefit her health.

T. '01—Rev. S. K. Emurian, Norfolk Presbytery evangelist, Suffolk, Va., has finished his work as field director of Near East Relief in North Carolina. According to officials of the organization, Mr. Emurian presented the message of Near East Relief more effectively than it had ever been presented before in the state, and the raising of at least $50,000 for the work is due to him. He received a letter of the highest appreciation from Josephus Daniels, former Secretary of the Navy, who is honorary state chairman of Near East Relief in North Carolina.

Ex-'02—Marcus Smythe, son of A. B..Smythe, was this year given the cup for being the best all-around student at University School, Cleveland. Last year his oldest brother was the winner of the cup.

'02-'03—Mrs. Anna H. Brown, mother of Albert Raffles Brown, '02, and Robert Elliott Brown, '03, died in Waterbury, Conn., on May 13. Both of the sons who graduated from Oberlin are Congregational ministers. Her other children include a third Congregational minister, a college professor, and a member of the Canadian Parliament.

'04—George R. Brown and Miss Elsie Louise Abring were married in Cleveland June 14.

'05—Jonathan M. Kurtz is professor of physics at Goshen College, Goshen, Ind.

'06—Ethel M. Kitch of the philosophy department of Oberlin College, and Chester H. Yeaton, assistant professor of mathematics, were married June 21. They are at home in Oberlin, where Mr. Yeaton is now teaching in the summer school.

'07—Abbie Miller Ogilvie (Mrs. Charles L.) has had articles on "Bandit Raids and China's Weakness" in recent issues of the *Christian Science Monitor* and the Boston *Transcript*. Mrs. Ogilvie returned to this country last August from Peking, China, where, with her husband, the Rev. Charles L. Ogilvie, she had been a missionary of the Presbyterian Board since 1911. Dr. Ogilvie was professor of Comparative Religion and Church History in Peking University until his death in 1919. Mrs. Ogilvie, with her two little sons, is making her home at present at 20 Orchard Street, Beverly, Mass.

T. '07-'08—Rev. John J. Banninga is secretary of the American Madura Mission, Pasumalai, S. India, now in its eighty-ninth year.

'08—While Mrs. Tracy Strong (Edith Robbins) was at the class reunion in Oberlin Tracy Strong was attending the third international conference for Y. M. C. A. workers among boys. The conference this year was held at Portschach, Austria.

'08—Mrs. A. J. Boynton (Ruth Bullock) after attending Commencement went on to Chautauqua where she and her family spend summers.

'08—Charles S. Kent died of appendicitis at Suffield, Ohio, on June 9.

'08—Mabel G. Whiting came from Santa Ana, Calif., to be present at the 15th anniversary of '08. She will spend the summer in Oberlin.

'09—The Night Law School of the University of Omaha recently published a bulletin on the Workmen's Compensation Law of Nebraska prepared by William M. Burton, who is an instructor in the school. The bulletin cites all decisions of the Supreme Court which in any way interpret the law. Mr. Burton's law offices are at 440 Peters Trust Bldg., Omaha.

'10—J. Vincent Durbin left Cincinnati last February and moved to Richmond, Ind., as manager of the R. F. Johnston Paint Company. His address is 15 N. Ninth Street.

'10—The new Presbyterian church of Pleasantville, N. Y., was opened and dedicated on Sunday, May 20. Rev. Lester H. Bent is pastor of the church.

'10-C. '13--Born, May 20, to Mr. and Mrs. Mark O. Ward (Gladys Dingfelder) of Toledo, Ohio, a son, Frederick Oscar.

'10-'18—In a national contest of high school bands held in Chicago under the direction of the Civic Music League convention, the boy's band of Fostoria, Ohio, high school, directed by John W. Wainwright, won the first place. The band receives a cash prize of $1,000 and instruments valued at about $800. On the occasion of the awarding of the prize Mr. Wainwright was decorated with a ribbon before an audience of 7,000 people and was allowed to conduct a massed band of competing organizations numbering 2,000 pieces.

'11—Robert E. Cushman has accepted a professorship in political science at Cornell University. His appointment fills the vacancy left by the death of Professor Samuel P. Orth. For the last four years Mr. Cushman has been in the department of political science at the University of Minnesota, three years as associate professor and last year as professor.

'11—Dr. Rhys P. Jones and Mrs. Jones (Marian Mortland, '11), with their two children, are now located at 717 Forest Ave., South Bend, Ind. Dr. Jones is pastor of the Westminster Presbyterian church of that city.

'11-'22—Dora Leonhard Van Alstine, '22, of Paterson, N. J., has announced her engagement to Hally Mering Scott, '11, of Tulsa, Okla.

'13—Rev. Philip D. Dutton is treasurer of the Taiku Church Building Fund in Shansi, China. He writes that the property wanted as a site for the new church has at last been secured, and that the material for building it will be obtained by wrecking two of the buildings just purchased. The members of the Taiku Station are very happy over what has so far been accomplished and hopeful regarding the prospect for securing the necessary funds.

'13—Bertha Alvera Miller passed away at Rockford City Hospital, Rockford, Ill., May 3, 1923. Death followed a mastoid operation, the trouble being brought on by complications of influenza.

Miss Miller was born in Rockford July 8, 1891, and attended Rockford high school and Rockford College, graduating from Oberlin College in 1913. Finishing her college work, she was a successful teacher in the Rockford schools for five years.

From her youth there had been the hope that she might sometime be a nurse; so she entered the Presbyterian Hospital School for Nurses in Chicago, graduating there in 1921. Her ability as a nurse was quickly recognized and she was put upon the nursing staff of the Presbyterian Hospital, serving in the capacity of special nurse. She was an active Christian and was untiring in her devotion to her work. More than one life despaired of by the physicians was saved by her persistent skillful care. Indeed she paid the last full measure of devotion in her service, for it was while caring for a pneumonia patient that she contracted the disease which caused her death. The hymn sung at her funeral, "O Master, let me walk with Thee in lowly paths of service free," expresses the spirit of her life.

Her marriage to Mr. Emery J. Carlson of Chicago was to have been an event of this fall. She is survived by her parents, Dr. and Mrs. T. N. Miller, and a sister, Mrs. H. W. Bais (Edith A. Miller, '04).

'13—At the commencement of Columbia University on June 6, Annie A. Bovie was granted the degree of Master of Arts in Mathematics.

'13—Dorothy Gunn, little daughter of Mr. and Mrs. J. Burns Gunn (Dorothy Rowe) of 2625 E. 130th St., Cleveland, died of pneumonia on May 21.

'13-'15—Mrs. Josephine Gammons Hammond, for the last five years Foreign Trade Secretary at the Cleveland Chamber of Commerce, has left for Shanghai, China, where she is to be a commercial agent of the United States government. She is the first woman to hold a position of this kind, the government having never before recognized a woman among its field officers.

'14—The Gorham Press, Boston, will issue at an early date "Neophytes," a volume of poems written by Miss Gladys Latchaw of Lansing, Mich. Miss Latchaw for three years was professor of English in Findlay College, Findlay, Ohio, and has been engaged recently in research work for the Children's Bureau of the United States Department of Labor. A second volume of verse has been completed and will be released later in the year.

'14—Born, to Mr. and Mrs. Harold M. Metcalf, June 2, in Cleveland, a son, Edward Irving.

'14—Theodore Reed, who has been for several years with the National Lumber and Manufacturing Company at Hoquiam, Wash., is now sales-manager of the Stout Lumber Company of Oregon, with headquarters at North Bend on Coos Bay.

'14—Gertrude R. Wheeler was married on May 11 to Mr. Franklyn Charles Scott at Colorado Springs, Colo.

'14—Florence Ada Pease was married on June 16 at the home of her mother in Berwyn, Ill., to Mr. Marshall Lewis Mathews. After August 1 her address will be 447 North Waiola Avenue, La Grange, Ill.

Ex-'14—Griffin McCarthy is general manager of the Famous and Barr Company of St. Louis, one of the largest department stores in the United States. Normally the store has 3,000 employees, and during the Christmas rush nearly 4,000.

'15—Harold Smith, having completed his graduate study in Paris with a recital, has accepted a professorship of organ and piano at Vassar College, where he replaces E. Harold Geer.

'15—Nathan L. Mack, formerly of the Roadside Settlement, Des Moines, Iowa, on June 1 took up the work of General Secretary of the Y. M. C. A. at Boone, Iowa.

'15—Dorothy Printup was married on June 16 to Professor Archer Butler Hulbert. The wedding took place at the home of her mother in Britton, S. Dak.

'15—Margaret Potter received her doctor's degree in psychology from Johns Hopkins University on June 12. She also was elected to Phi Beta Kappa from among six possible candidates in her department.

C.'15-'16—Mary E. Helman has resigned her position as director of the music department of Fisk University in order to go on with her study of music. She is to be succeeded by Mrs. Mabel Starkey, also a former student in the Oberlin Conservatory, who has been in charge of the school music department of Grinnell College. During her four years at Fisk, Miss Helman had one great aim: that of convincing the world that colored people can sing the music of the great masters as well as their own folk songs. Her faith in her pupils and her tireless efforts were supremely justified on April 26 and 27 by the rendition of the cantata "King Olaf," under her direction, by the Mozart Society of Fisk University, a chorus of 53 girls and 25 young men. The performance was so remarkable that it drew from the musical critics of the state, hitherto unconvinced, the concession that the negro has the power of interpreting classic music as adequately as the great artists of other races.

T. '15-'17—Born, April 8, to Mr. and Mrs.

George W. Webber of Des Moines, Iowa, a second son, Robert Loren. Mr. Webber is Associate General Secretary of the Y. M. C. A. in Des Moines.

'16—Amy F. Webster will spend the summer at Mammoth Springs Camp, Yellowstone Park.

'16—Bert H. McQueer, who has just finished a course at Boston Tech., has accepted a position with the National Carbon Company in Cleveland.

'16—Rossleene M. Arnold has been awarded the Cutler Fellowship in Physiological Chemistry at Yale University for 1923-24.

'16—Lawrence T. Wyly, formerly first lieutenant, 48th Aero Squadron, was awarded the Distinguished Service Cross of the United States army on June 7, at Fort Snelling, Minn. The presentation was made by Major General George N. Duncan, commander of the Seventh Army Corps area. Lieutenant Wyly is cited for exceptional bravery in three engagements: one on August 15, 1918, near Chaules, in which he successfully led a flight of five American planes against twenty enemy planes, landing just behind the American lines with his plane riddled with bullets; the second on September 17, near Cambrai, when he dispersed five enemy planes single-handed; and the third on October 21, when he and a companion attacked and threw into turmoil a two-mile enemy transport column, again barely making the American lines before his plane collapsed. Lieutenant Wyly's address is 715 University Avenue, S. E., Minneapolis, Minn.

'16—Leonard P. Bennett has established a new magazine, the Inter-Lake Weekly, published at 321½ Huron Street, Toledo, Ohio. The magazine is "a survey of commercial progress in Toledo and the Lake region."

Ex-'17—Amos N. Wilder is the author of "Battle Retrospect and Other Poems," published by the Yale University Press.

'17—Dorothy E. Wright has left Madisonville, Ky., and has accepted a position in Georgetown, Ky., as Supervising Nurse of the Scott County Health Department. Her address is 138 South Hamilton Street, Georgetown.

'17—Elbert M. Shelton is the holder of the Cheney fellowship for investigation in the chemistry of silk at Yale University for next year.

'18—Born to Mr. and Mrs. J. W. Quinton (Marianne E. Kirk), on January 28, a daughter, Katherine Kirk Quinton.

'18—While J. Hollis Harmon was leaning over a fence, which guarded a cliff back of his temporary home in Seattle, the supports gave way and pitched him down on the rocks twelve feet below, from which he rolled about sixty feet to the bottom of the declivity. When help came it was found that his nose and both legs were broken. While recovering in the hospital he was operated on for appendicitis.

'18—Benjamin L. Pierce has been elected superintendent of schools for Erie County, Ohio. There were fourteen candidates for the position. Mr. Pierce has been superintendent of schools in Huron, Ohio, for four years, and was principal of the high school there the preceding year.

'18—Rene L. Smith of Hecla, S. D., was married on May 19 to Mme. Marie Lambert of Montpellier, France. Mr. Smith has been an instructor in the Oberlin high school for the last two years. Mrs. Smith has already returned to France, and he expects to join her there this summer.

'18-'20—John H. Jameson and Leontine Wright were married June 2 in Dayton at the home of Miss Katharine Wright and Orville Wright, aunt and uncle of the bride. They are now at home at 1388 Hall Avenue, Cleveland.

'18—Ford E. Curtis, who for two years has been instructor in English at Case School of Applied Science, Cleveland, will go to Columbia University next fall to begin work for a master's degree.

Ex '18-ex '19—Theodore N. Bates, ex '18, and Mrs. Bates, (Pauline Gladys Barrett) ex '19, have moved from Elyria, Ohio, to 3787 W. 139th Street, Cleveland, Ohio. Mr. Bates is now with the Cleveland Plain Dealer classified advertising department.

'19—Joseph W. Ellis received his doctor's degree in physics from the University of California in May. For the coming year he has accepted an instructorship in the Southern Branch of the University of California, in Los Angeles.

'19-'20—Mary Louise Finch and Howard Hall were married at Oberlin June 21. Miss Finch, who has been a member of the faculty of Ripon College, Wis., for the past two years, received the degree of M.A. from that institution at the recent commencement. Mr. Hall graduated this year from the Harvard University Law School. Mr. and Mrs. Hall will reside in Cleveland, where Mr. Hall will engage in the practice of law.

'20—Robert S. Fletcher has been appointed head assistant in the American History department at Harvard University for the coming year.

A.M. '20-'21—Born, May 26, to Mr. and Mrs. Ralph Brewster Noyce (Harriet Norton) of Denmark, Iowa, a son, Donald Sterling.

'21—Kathryn Knowlton receives her master's degree in chemistry at the University of Chicago this year. Next year she will teach in Hollins College, Hollins, Va.

'21—Helen P. Groves and Ezra T. Hazeltine were married June 7 at Ludlow, Pa. They are now at home at South Bend, Wash.

'21—Harlan G. ("Goldie") Metcalf has resigned as coach at Case School of Applied Science, Cleveland, and will take post graduate work at Columbia University next year. He will be succeeded at Case by Arthur Winters, '23.

'22—Born, May 13, to Mr. and Mrs. Arthur W. Andrews, of Kamehameha School, Honolulu, Hawaii, a daughter, Marion Elizabeth.

'22—Award of a Public Health Fellowship in Chemistry at Northwestern University goes again to the last year's holder, Henry Bent.

'22—Mr. and Mrs. George Van Bockern of Bluff City, Tenn., have announced the engagement of their daughter, Ella Evadne, to Mr. John H. Longborn of Valley City, Ohio. For the past year Miss Van Bockern has taught science in the Columbia, Ohio, high school.

Ex-'22—Born, May 28, to Mr. and Mrs. Wilbur I. Newstetter (Jessie Hayden, ex-'22), a son, Wilbur I., Jr.

Several news items about recent graduates have been held over for the October issue.

Oberlin Kindergarten-Primary Training School

A two-year course preparing for kindergarten and primary teaching. Dormitories. Expenses moderate. An accredited school with national patronage.

FOR CATALOGUE ADDRESS

Miss Rose Dean, 125 Elm Street, Oberlin, Ohio

WHATEVER your "Choice of a Career", college training has increased your economic value. In any business or profession, adequate life insurance is a proper self-appraisal of value to the State, the family and yourself. The traditions, practices and financial strength of the John Hancock Life Insurance Company are such that you can take genuine pride in a John Hancock policy on your life. It is a distinct asset.

Should you desire to go into a satisfactory business for yourself—to build your own business with the aid of a strong organization, to secure substantial remuneration in return for hard, intelligent work—then it will pay you to sell John Hancock Insurance.

We invite inquiry from you regarding a possible career or an adequate John Hancock policy on your life.

Address Agency Department

John Hancock

LIFE INSURANCE COMPANY
OF BOSTON, MASSACHUSETTS

*Sixty-one Years
in Business*

*Largest Fiduciary Institution
in New England*

Summer Vacation Reading

We offer you our services while on your vacation to furnish you with reading matter.

We suggest books of travel, latest fiction or a book of poems.

Write us for catalogues of suitable summer reading.

We can obtain any book published for your requirements.

A. G. COMINGS & SON

37 WEST COLLEGE ST.   OBERLIN, OHIO

OBERLIN C

OBERLIN, O

HENRY CHURCHILL KI

The Ideal of th

" That Oberlin may be as good a college
apologize for no element in its life or work
than quantity; putting first things first; ma
all parts of its work, so that its degree may
nates may take pride; that it may continu
individuality; and that as a part of this in
continue to stand for courage, for convicti
that gives world-vision and prepares for worl

The Ninety-first Year will begin Wednes

Admission to the College of Arts and Scienc
mission of freshmen and advanced standing stude
mission of *women* were assigned April 1st.

The total number of new places for *men* in
the freshman class, 175; advanced standing, 25.
six places for men with advanced standing remain
tion should be made to the Secretary of the Col

Admission to the Conservatory of Music.
Conservatory of Music are now being received.
places for first year students have been assigne
ply for entrance blanks to the Secretary of the Co

The Ohio State Mortgage Company

CLEVELAND, OHIO

8% Tax Exempt, Cumulative Preferred Stock

The Ohio State Mortgage Company was organized in February, 1916, with a capital of $10,000. The company buys short time mortgage notes at a discount, and either holds them until maturity or sells them at a profit. The company also makes first mortgage construction loans, and collateral loans secured by mortgages. Each mortgage is secured by a much greater amount in real estate. The capital stock of The Ohio State Mortgage Company is non-assessable and is exempt from State, County and Municipal taxes. Dividends are exempt from the normal Federal Income Tax. Every share issued was paid for in full, none was given away, nor will any be given away.

FINANCIAL CONDITION

The following statement shows the financial strength of the company:

	Authorized	Issued
Common Stock	$1,000,000	$631,300
8% Preferred Stock	1,000,000	319,600
Total Authorized Capital	$2,000,000	$950,900
Assets of the company as of March 15th, 1923		$1,200,489.92
Regular annual dividend on common stock since 1916		10%
Extra dividends on common stock since 1916		25%
Regular annual dividend on preferred stock		8%

MANAGEMENT

DIRECTORS	ADVISORY BOARD	EXECUTIVE OFFICERS
Robb O. Bartholomew	Florence E. Allen	Robb O. Bartholomew, President
J. H. Bromelmeier	Thomas A. Cheney	
L. T. Goodwin	Dan Dimmick	
John E. Grady	Chas. Ehrich	Brennan B. West, Vice-President
Joseph Maca	C. M. Goodwin	
David P. Maclure	Fred G. Miller	
Harry Rider	John G. Osmond	John R. Watson, Secretary and Manager
Brennan B. West	Joseph D. Paterson	
John R. Watson	C. H. Pratt	
	Azariah S. Root	L. T. Goodwin, Treasurer
	Norman E. Shaw	
	H. F. Vaughan	

The stock can be purchased at $100 per share for cash, or 20% cash and 2% monthly. On partial payments the company will pay 6% interest on the amount credited to the purchaser if made according to the terms on the application. Dividends from earnings begin from date of subscription.

Oberlin, Ohio — Habel-Keiser-Severy Investment Company.

Warren, Ohio — Karl B. King & Company, Robins Theatre Bldg.

Ashtabula, Ohio — H. H. Timby.

Erie, Pa. — Frank L. Maclure, 1008 Palace Hardware Bldg.

David P. Maclure
541 Engineers Bldg.
Cleveland, Ohio

Lightning Source UK Ltd.
Milton Keynes UK
UKHW012330061118
331891UK00010B/975/P